D1860311

WHY GODSE KILLED GANDHI ?

WHY GODES KILLED GANDHI ?

WHY GODSE KILLED GANDHI ?

V.T. RAJSHEKAR

GYAN PUBLISHING HOUSE
New Delhi - 110002

WHY GODSE KILLED GANDHI ?

ISBN :9788121212977

Rs. 350

© V.T. Rajshekar

All rights reserved. No part of this book may be reproduced in any manner without written permission.

Published in 2014 in India by
Gyan Publishing House
23, Ansari Road, Daryaganj,
New Delhi - 110002
Phones : 23261060, 23282060 Fax : 23285914
e-mail : books@gyanbooks.com
website : gyanbooks.com

Laser Typesetting at : Vinayak Printers, Delhi
Printed at : Salasar Imaging System, Delhi

CONTENTS

FOREWORD

This is the second revised edition of our hit book. Published in 1983, it proved an instant success and sold out in two years. No other book published by the Dalit Sahitya Akademy has become so popular with every section of the society as this tiny book. Its publication coincided with the release of the *Gandhi* film running to packed houses in world capitals and so the book became topical too. The book answered the star question deliberately left unanswered in the film. The book not only became popular in India but also outside. It was translated to Japanese and created a sensation in Japan and other parts of the world. The book also came out in Tamil, Malayalam, Telugu and Kannada. Other languages will soon follow.

Those who read this book said this was the first time they were getting a truthful picture of Gandhi and Nathuram Godse, the killer of the *Mahatma*. They also said that the book came as a real shock to them. Because it came out with many a closely guarded secret.

All these prove that the people are hungering for facts which are hidden by the rulers of India. This ruling class takes a vow everyday saying *satya mewa jayate* (truth shall triumph) but in action it does everything to murder truth and finish anybody speaking the truth. At the time of writing this, we are facing a sedition charge for speaking the truth, perhaps the first person in the State of Karnataka to face this charge.

Because of the big demand for the book, we thought of this revised edition reinforced with many more evidences. We are sure this new book will help inquiring minds- so rare in India - wanting to separate myths from reality.

A pleasant surprise is that neither the Gandhi admirers nor the Godse godfathers took offence at this book (first edition). Not at least till the time of writing this. This shows that the book is not intended to hurt anybody's feelings and that even the book's worst critics have appreciated our arguments - again a very rare thing in India.

Gandhi is India's most revered figure and anybody

criticising him is considered a bloody fool. We too respect Gandhi and acknowledge his contributions. But a society interested in scientific and technological progress cannot live on myths alone. Those blind admirers of Gandhi must know that Mao Tse-tung is held in greater esteem in China than Gandhi here. But the Chinese had the moral courage to publicly criticise Mao and re-assess his contributions. It is this forward-looking values of China that made it a world power, where as India is languishing.

India's value system makes the Indians believe in myths and not the reality. The tragedy of Gandhi is that India's ruling class accepted the social and political part of gandhism rejecting the better part of his "philosophy" namely his economic theories. Jayaprakash Narayan, considered a great gandhian leader, once said that gandhism is better practised in China than in India. India accepted Gandhi's political and social philosophy because it suited its people. The "gandhian economics" was against the interests of its ruling class and that is why it was rejected without saying so. The "gandhian economics" laying stress on rural development, small is beautiful, cottage industry, self-reliance, simple living - all these cut at the very root of our urban-dwelling upper caste rulers. Not one person in India speaks about the "gandhian economics" except Charan Singh and for advocating it he is called mad. If the Hindu rulers of India had so much love for Gandhi, why did they reject the best part of gandhism and hugged only the worst part of it? It is all hypocrisy.

Gandhi is the forgotten man of India. A pathetic figure. No school or college anywhere in India has a textbook on Gandhi or gandhism. In China, Mao's *Red Book* containing his Thoughts is a must for every child. In India, there is no demand for Gandhi's books. (He has written perhaps only one book, *An Autobiography-My Experiments with Truth*) which itself is a collection of articles written in his journal and later translated to English and published as a book. IAS and IPS (civil service) examinations have no questions on Gandhi. And yet Gandhi's photo is there in every government office in India. The numerous books of Gandhi (all collection of his dull and drab articles and speeches) found in libraries are gathering dust. If his name is mentioned by a speaker in any city convent where fashionable girls study, it will evoke a derisive laughter. The *Gandhi Jayanti* (his birth anniversary day - Oct. 2) is now an official function where some old bandicoots reluctantly gather and deliver some hypocritical speeches sitting inside a closed room. Within an hour or so, it is all over. Compared to that, Dr. Babasaheb Ambedkar's *Jayanti* (April 14) is a massive, day-long, open-air celebration attended by thousands of Dalits spending their own money. The celebrations go on for at least three months.

That doesn't mean Gandhi has lost his place. Since he symbolises the typical Indian hypocrisy, his name has to be mentioned in every speech. No speech will be complete without quoting or misquoting Gandhi. Every leader calls upon the youth to "emulate" Gandhi but we have not come across any interest in today's youth to follow him.

That also doesn't mean we are maligning Gandhi. Nor are we interested in maligning a community or any individual. My own lawyer in my *Indian Express* dismissal case is a Brahmin-M.C. Narasimhan, of the Communist Party of India (CPI). Our criticism is directed against an oppressive system which is responsible for the violence that is bleeding India at all ends. There are good people in every caste, community or religion. Vagabondism is not the monopoly of any caste or group. A people poised for leap into the 21st century cannot depend upon vagabonds. The "educated" upper caste rulers must learn to listen to criticisms and correct themselves. If not, they will be forcibly made to correct themselves.

We have spent enough time quarreling. Ever since "independence" we have been busy only quarreling, cutting each other's throat. For this inherent weakness in us, our value system is solely responsible. There will be no peace, no progress as long as India's "majority community" of Hindus does not get rid of this dangerous value system. Indians, and the Hindus in particular, would have destroyed their value system had it really harmed them. But the very fact they are clinging to it, whether upper or lower castes, from centuries shows that they have been profited by this value system - despite the fact that the entire country today is steeped in corruption, violence and a grab mentality. They love this value system because it has given them full scope to exploit. If this exploitation has to stop, this value system has to be destroyed.

If Gandhi or gandhism is attacked, do you know who is going to pounce upon you like a mad dog and bite you all over? It is this corrupt lot. And most of them Hindu zealots who have perfected the art of saying one thing and doing exactly the opposite of it. Our Hindu leaders say the whole world is *maya* (myth) and as such we should not covet private gain. Material gain is an illusion, they say. But it is only those who propagate this philosophy, who rob the weak. Nowhere in the world exploitation of the weak and the women is done with such perfect fineness as in India by giving it a religious touch. The Birlas, the country's largest business house in whose mansion Gandhi died, are India's most ardent temple-builders. And how this business house acquired all its wealth can be found from the government's own documents. Our priests are so much worried about personal hygiene that they have to take bath at the very sight of an Untouchable. But how these priests keep the temples can be seen by a visit to Kashi and Tirupati, our two "holiest" of the holy temples. We call the Ganga as the holiest river -a dip in which would purify us of all our sins. But we have given the contract to purify the Ganga water stinking with dead bodies and sewage to a French firm.

Nowhere in the world the word "peace", "non-violence", "tolerance" and "brotherhood" are repeated so many times a day as in India. But nowhere in the world so much blood is shed. Perhaps more people were killed in India after the "independence" than in the two World Wars. We talk of "democracy", "equality before law" but keep a third of India's 800-million people as Untouchables, unseeables, unapproachables and unthinkables. Our courts have one set of law for the poor and another for the rich. A poor starving man if he steals a fowl, he is called a thief, handcuffed and beaten up in the police station. But a business magnate who evades tax for years gets a "national award". Our police are called the law and order enforcing agency but in many places they have become the single biggest threat to law and order.

It is no longer Hindu-Muslim riots now but Hindu police-Muslim riots. The elections are a farce.

India is the only country in the world which has perfected the art of double-think and double-cross as a fine art. This is the direct result of our value system.

But this value system derived from Hinduism is not only responsible for this persecution of Untouchables, Tribals, backward class shudras, its religious minorities, its women but it has also harmed many Brahmins themselves. Brahmins all over India raise a hue and cry that there are any number of "poor" among them and, therefore, all selections should be done on the basis of "economic criterion". If such a value system does not benefit its own creators, what then is its use? That means even the Brahmins have a duty to work for the destruction of this value system.

A set of values cherished by a society does not go by what is described as "change of heart". It can be destroyed only when that society plunges into a revolution which gives birth to a new set of values.

The moment we talk about revolution, the stock reply we get is: Where is the leader to lead us to such a revolution? Can anybody produce a leader? No. A leader is never made. There is nothing like a born leader. The leader emerges when the situation becomes ripe. The people's collective need for freedom throws up a leader. As Louis Farrakhan, the famous Black leader from USA, welcoming Gaddafi at the Second Mathaba Conference, Libya, on March 15, 1986 said: "A leader is produced out of the longing and need of the people". (*Dalit Voice*, April 16, '86). When a people are oppressed, it is the need for freedom that produces a longing which in turn produces a leader. That means a leader is the product of a collective necessity. The people will never be free until they produce such a leader with the vision to create the revolution and see it through its logical end.

So, the condition for such a revolution is oppression. India has not reached that stage of oppression. And we have a doubt if the whole sub-continent of India will be subjected to such an oppression. The Sikhs and Nagas are undergoing that oppression. The Muslims may be heading towards greater oppression. But the Dalits have not reached that stage. Since India is not a nation but a group of nations, each nation may have to have its own revolution. The country as a whole may not see such a single revolution. This is because a vast majority of this country are victims not of violence but non-violence. The slaves all over the world are fighting against violence inflicted upon them by their respective ruling class. But in India, there is no fight - let alone an armed struggle - because they are killed not by violence but by non-violence. India is the only example of its kind in the whole world and Gandhi's contribution to this state of affairs is not small.

All those interested in revolution in India including its "poor" Brahmins must create conditions for such a revolution. When such a revolutionary situation develops and the oppression reaches unbearable heights, a leader is automatically thrown up.

So, this book should be considered by all those yearning for revolution as our contribution to crate such a desire for revolution. Godse pushed India towards that revolution which Gandhi checkmated.

I am indebted to many friends including Iqbal Ahmed Sheriff, Advocate, Bangalore, for supplying me with lot of material and my son Salil for going through the proof.

Bangalore
July, 1, 1986

V.T. RAJSHEKAR

FOREWORD

FOR THE THIRD REVISED EDITION

1. As this is written the Aryan rulers are busy preparing for the 50th anniversary of India's independence. They are making it such a deafening song and dance event not only in India but the world over - to frighten the innocent victims who have been bypassed by their "independence" (1947) inside India and to bamboozle the world outside about India bursting into "world's largest working democracy". Who are we to object to the entertainment of the rulers? The "independence" has benefitted the Aryans and made them the rulers. Hence they have every right to celebrate such a smooth operation. Should they not celebrate such a *Ram Rajya* - heaven on earth - assured by their "Father of the Nation"? But the over 85% of the country's 1,000 million population comprising its indigenous (*Bahujans*) masses plus the women of the ruling class itself have nothing to be proud of this "independence" which might have brought the country self-rule but at the cost of our self-respect.

2. The country is 50 years old. And at this age, a person or society is expected to attain maturity, some amount of wisdom, self-confidence, status and dignity. Did India acquire all these? Not only India failed miserably on all these fronts but acquired the dubious distinction of being called a begger nation — a laughing stock of the whole world. Every Asian country which became "independent" much later has overtaken India. Who created this mess? Not we, the critics of M.K. Gandhi, but his followers. This book narrates this sad Truth and also expresses our agony that the rulers of India are in no mood to know the Truth - as any effort to pause and ponder will slow down their race to exploit the indigenous Indians.

3. The greatest casualty in today's India - during this golden jubilee — is the Truth. They are so much intoxicated by their 50-year non-stop exploitation that they have failed to see that they have killed Justice and Truth and instead sold injustice and falsehood. Do they know the cost of such a murder of Truth and Justice? No. Because they have not only become intoxicated but also blind. Fortunately, their number is small and the others, over 85% of the natives, are free from this lunacy. So, what is said in this book may be called stupid, nonsense, exaggerated, malicious, vile propaganda and polemics, if not downright bullshit. Incendiary? But this country belongs to us and we have the right to say what according to us is Justice and Truth. Aryan rulers are settlers here. And it is they who made a mess of our country. We have to correct it and bring back these Aryans to sanity. This is the message of the book.

4. It was in this book that we first propounded the theory of "Sacred Brahmins" vs. the "Socialist Brahmins" which later culminated into the *Dialogue of the Bhoodevatas* (Dalit Sahitya Akademy, 1993). No person involved in public life, particularly the Dalits and the persecuted nationalities denied human rights, can afford to ignore this grand drama – the mock battle between the two sections of Aryans - which has been entertaining and befooling us and will continue to do so. Hence the importance of this book as it unravels a wonderful but dangerous strategy that has kept the indigenous Bahujans divided and the Aryans as rulers.

5. Ever since we first wrote this book (1983) praising the "Sacred Brahmins" as our honest, open enemies and denouncing the "Socialist Brahmins" as dangerous and deadly enemies of the Bahujans, our people have launched not only an all-out war against the latter but lately formed a coalition government in Uttar Pradesh with the Hindu nazi political party of "Sacred Brahmins". This is an entirely new development in "independent" India and this working arrangement may be extended further. The coalition of the Bahujan Samaj Party (BSP) of Dalits and the Bharatiya Janata Party (BJP) of nazis is a natural outcome of the sharpening caste contradictions and the consequent all-round confusions that is India today. The thinking sections among the Aryans are worried because the Bahujans are not only becoming conscious but also growing angry. And this is sure to lead to some explosion. The rulers know it. They are not only the rulers but also the property-holders.

And they see a clear threat not only to their property but to their very existence. And in their desperate bid to save their lives, they are likely to compromise with a part of their property and power. In search of security, the "Sacred Brahmins" among Aryans are driven to seek shelter under the Bahujans. We have clearly forseen such a possibility. (*Dalit Voice* Editorial, Feb. 1, 1997: *"Desperate vaidiks plan national poll pact with Dalit parties for their survival"*). Even an all-India electoral pact with the "Sacred Brahmins", is not ruled out and the tumultuous social forces may make such a pact inevitable and unavoidable. But the problem with the Aryans is that the number of "Sacred Brahmins" is dwindling. The Hindu nazi party itself is fast giving up its "Socialist Brahmin" character. This is a dangerous sign. Hence this book is a warning to Aryans, particularly their *vaidik* brains, that the Bahujans are prepared to assure the Aryans their human rights provided they stick to their "Sacred Brahmin" character.

Bangalore
Date:Aug. 1, 1997

V.T. RAJSHEKAR

I - GODSE'S DEVOTION TO DUTY

The internationally-acclaimed British-made, multi-million dollar film, *Gandhi*, begins and ends with the pistol shot fired by Nathuram Godse, a Rashtriya Swayamsevak Sangh (RSS) Hindu nazi para-military force leader, killing M.K. Gandhi described by the Hindus as the "Father of the Nation", but it does not say why he was killed. The film generated so much of interest in Mohandas Karamchand Gandhi, hailing from a princely family, in India and abroad but we have not come across any report or discussion on why he was killed. The Hindu genius is to keep silent when the question is inconvenient. But the answer to this question is found in the Pune Chitpavan Brahmin, Godse's own book explaining in 122 pages why he killed Gandhi.

The book, *May It Please Your Honour*, reportedly banned, was published first in 1977 by his younger brother, Gopal Godse, (Vitasta Prakashan, 1206/1-B, J.M. Road, Pune-411 004-India, Rs. 15). The book has since run into several editions and secretly circulated among thousands of Godse admirers in India and abroad. The book is so forcefully argued that anybody reading it will get fully convinced that what Godse did was right. One cannot but appreciate the Brahmin Godse's devotion to his cause, brahminism, and his sincerity to defend it even at the cost of his life. Godse said he killed Gandhi because Gandhi had vowed that India would be divided over his dead body but secretly joined the conspiracy to partition India.

Honest Brahmins: That India should remain undivided (*Akhand Bharat*) was the firm stand of orthodox Brahmins like Godse who were honest to their cause of brahminism. But the problem was that their number was dwindling even at the time of Godse. The very concept of *Akhand Bharat* (undivided India which includes Pakistan and Bangladesh) has been given a goodbye even by the Hindu nazi party of RSS and its political arm, Bharatiya Janata Party (BJP) long back. Not a single Hindu nazi leader, including the head of the RSS, called *Sarasanghchalak*, talks about *Akhand Bharat* today.

L.K. Advani, a Sindhi migrant from Pakistan and president of the BJP, was once pulled up by the RSS for even casually referring to *Akhand Bharat* during his infamous *Ram Rath Yatra* that led to the destruction of Babri Masjid which in turn led to the destruction of Hindu nazi party itself. He was asked to shut up and none dare speak about *Akhand Bharat* later.

The point is no Brahmin or no upper caste (ruling class) leader today wants unity of the sub-continent (*Akhand Bharat*). Because the rulers know their interests. If the Muslims of Pakistan and Bangladesh are to rejoin India, the already shaking Aryan (upper caste) position will further suffer with the unity of Dalits, Muslims and Backward Castes which is fast consolidating into a mighty *Bahujan Samaj* movement.

In a united India the Aryan population, now at mere 15%, would further shrink to 5% and the Muslim population now at 15% would soar to 30% and Dalit population at 30% to 40%.

Godse belongs to that vanishing tribe of honest Brahmins and as this is written, about 50 years after Godse killed Gandhi, their tribe is practically nil.

Muslim opposition to partition: Partition of India brought immense benefit to the Aryan upper castes, particularly the *vaidiks* who became the ruling class of India. If India was not partitioned then there was no question of a *vaidik* (Jawaharlal Nehru) becoming the first Prime Minister of India and the brahminical exploitation reaching its climax. The credit for transferring the power from the British to the Brahmins, by cunningly avoiding the Muslim hindrance through partition, goes to none else but Gandhi.

That is how the practical-minded *vaidiks* led by Nehru goaded Gandhi to secretly support partition though as a typical Hindu Gandhi spoke one thing but acted against it. Gandhi quietly schemed at partition and the honest Brahmin in Godse mistook Gandhi believing his words that Gandhi was sincerely against partition though in fact he colluded in dividing India and that is why Godse killed him.

Muslims blamed for partition: The Hindus (Aryans) have made everybody believe that Gandhi was against the partition of India and successfully sold the falsehood that it was the Muslims who caused partition of their mother land (*Bharat Mata*). The Aryan puzzle is that when the Hindus say "yes" they mean "no". Only if you are a master of the law of contradictions you can solve this puzzle. But the Aryan rulers have kept not only over 85% of the original inhabitants of India as illiterate but also fully confused and funky. The rulers have created a country of unthinking people. Not only they have suppressed the truth on partition but sold a damn lie as supreme truth - that it was the Muslims who caused the partition of India - and thereby severed the right and left arms of their *Bharat Mata*. This is the greatness, if it can be called greatness, of the Aryans that they can convert day into night and night into day.

So, in such an atmosphere it is the crooks who rule and these crooks manufacture falsehoods and sell it as supreme truth. One such myth is Gandhi and the myth of his opposition to partition.

The *Hindu* puts out truth: The Aryan rulers once in a way do put out the truth vaguely and also see to it that no eye catches it. And such sensitive informations are not given much publicity. If the victims of the Aryan oppressors are careful enough, it will be possible to get enough material to find out the truth.

And one such truth was found in the *Hindu*, India's chief brahminical daily (June 16, 1997), which reproduced the All-India Congress Committee debate on partition, published in its edition of June 16, 1947 - 50 years ago:

AICC debate on partition proposal

The All-India Congress Committee met in New Delhi on June 14 and inconclusively discussed the Working Committee's resolution to accept the British Government's plan announced on June 3 to divide India before granting freedom.

The resolution to approve the Working Committee's acceptance decision was moved by Pandit Govind Ballabh Pant and seconded by Maulana Abul Kalam Azad. Most of the 18 leaders who spoke opposed the Working Committee's decision. Mahatma Gandhi appealed for support to the stand taken by the Working Committee - lest, as he put it, world opinion go against the Congress.

Belying expectations that the Working Committee's stand would be approved by the AICC without trouble, strong criticism emerged in the debate forcing the discussions to be continued the next day. Observers, however, said the AICC's approval would yet be secured as both Gandhiji and the Congress president, Acharya Kripalani, had pointed out that an adverse vote would mean throwing the Congress Working Committee out of office.

Pandit Pant analysed the good points in the scheme such as immediate dominion status, freedom to build up a strong dynamic Centre and a democratic system in the Provinces without separate electorates, as also weightage in the Legislative and Services. He seemed confident that the secession of certain parts of India would prove temporary. Maulana Azad commended the scheme on the ground that any solution then was far better than drifting towards further chaos.

Among the many speakers who opposed the British Plan, Dr. Choithram Gidwani, president of the Sind Congress Committee, expressed the deep anxiety of non-Muslims in Muslim majority areas. Babu Purushothamdas Tandon, in his repeatedly cheered speech, criticised the Congress for having surrendered to the Muslim League and to Britain without in any way making certain that communal strife would cease. He asked the AICC to reject the British Plan observing that it was not the prestige of the members of the Working Committee that was at stake, but the future of the whole country.

Building on falsehood: This above document makes it clear that Gandhi did favour partition.

But it is for the rulers to ponder what will happen to their own children if they are fed on a diet of falsehood. Can they build a future on falsehood?

That is how the grateful ruling class has kept Gandhi's portrait in all govt. offices, courts and particularly police stations.

Aryan rulers and the Hindu nazis in particular might have given up the idea of *Akhand Bharat* but the oppressed over 85% of India's population is hungering for such a united India (*Dalit Voice*: Dec. 16, 1990: Ishaq M.J. Godhrawala, Bombay: *"Akhand Bharat idea gains ground"*, and *Dalit Voice* Jan. 16, 1991 p.23: *"Akhand Bharat with autonomy for each nation"*, *Dalit Voice* March 1, 1991 p.17: *"Confederation of Indian sub-continent with full autonomy for each nationality"*). The idea of a "United States of India" (USI) comprising India, Pakistan and Bangladesh is growing not only in India but in other two countries also.

Greatness of Godse: The greatness of Godse is that he never hides his intentions. His book, therefore, is in sharp contrast to the tongue-in-cheek utterances of present-day RSS leaders and other "Sacred Brahmins" or honest Brahmin leaders who have departed from their strict *vedic* traditions and started concealing brahminism under a mask of marxism. Poor Godse did not live to see how his own honest Brahmin tribe sold away its honesty in search of quick gains. The RSS itself has stopped talking of the *Bunch of Thoughts* book and even stopped selling it, if not disowning it. Today's Hindu nazi party leaders are no longer honest *vaidiks* like Golwalkar or Godse. They have compromised their principles for worldly pleasures, posts, positions and perks.

Hence Godse can be considered as one of the sincerest disciples of Guru Golwalkar, the chief Hindu nazi ideologue and the author of the RSS bible, *Bunch of Thoughts*. (II ed. revised-1980- Jagran Prakashan, Kempe Gowda Nagar, Bangalore-560 019, Rs.30).

The Godse book, *May It Please Your Honour*, is the statement made by him in the court. He does not address Gandhi as *mahatma* (great) although this title was given to Gandhi by the grateful Brahmins for the great services rendered to brahminism and for helping to drive out the British imperialism and replacing it with the more gory brahminical imperialism. All those who are interested in studying brahminism and how the "Brahmin mind" works should know how a set of people, whom some people describe as the "Jews of India", made use of Gandhi and finally shot him dead and after killing him adopted gandhism as the philosophy of India's ruling class. Gandhism has become the other name for Hinduism, put in a sugar-coated pill,so that India's persecuted nationalities like Muslims, Christians, Sikhs etc. swallow it with pleasure. (V.T. Rajshekar: *Hinduism, Fascism, Gandhism*-DSA, 1985, Rs.5).

Brahmin hatred of Muslims: Some Hindu leaders had criticised Dr. Babasaheb Ambedkar, the leader of India's vast Untouchables, for addressing the *mahatma* merely as "Mr. M.K. Gandhi" but the Brahmin Godse who killed Gandhi to protect Hinduism did not even use the word "Mr". The Brahmin rule says that what they do is right and what others do is wrong. Who is to punish them? They are the thief, police, prosecutor, judge, jailor and hangman - all put in one.

The Government of India constituted a special court headed by Atma Charan Agarwal, ICS, and it sat in the historic Red Fort, Delhi. There were 12 accused including "Veer" Savarkar, also a Brahmin described by the RSS as a great nationalist and architect of the *Hindutva*, the doctrine of brahminical racial supremacy, in whose house in Bombay the conspiracy to kill Gandhi was hatched.

Godse's book is perhaps the most authentic documentary evidence to date to prove the extent of Brahmin hatred of the Muslims. Islam and brahminism are like serpent and mongoose (M.N. Roy: *Historical Role of Islam*, 1981 reprint, Ajanta Publication 1 U-B, Jawahar Nagar, Bungalow Road, New Delhi-110 007, Rs.30).

Hinduism as nationalism: Present-day Hindu nazi leaders may praise Gandhi for their own selfish reasons and their political party (BJP) might have once adopted gandhism as its political philosophy, but Godse has clearly stated that Gandhi was anti-Hindu and in India anybody who is anti-Hindu automatically becomes anti-national. Because, the "national" media, fully controlled by *vaidik* forces, has made the reading public believe that Hinduism is nationalism and vice versa. The Sikh struggle for self-determination was met with military might in 1984 by launching a "Blue Star Operation" in which over 3,000 innocent Sikhs were killed in the Golden Temple, Amritsar.

False interpretation of *Gita*: An unsigned introduction to Godse's book says Gandhi's views on the *Gita* are erroneous and differs from the authentic interpretation given by Bala Gangadhar Tilak, also a Chitpavan Brahmin from Pune (*Two Brahmins from Poona*, pages 359 to 375 in the book, *Freedom at Midnight*, by Collins and Lapierre.)

Gandhi's interpretation of the *Gita* was false, according to a "great gandhian", D.K. Gosavi, whose book, *Tilak, Gandhi & Gita* (1983), published by India's premier brahminical publishing house, Bharatiya Vidya Bhavan, Bombay, founded by a Gujarati top Brahmin leader, K.M. Munshi. According to Gosavi, also a Brahmin, Tilak's interpretation of the *Gita* is exactly on the lines of Shankarachari (788 - 820 AD). Tilak's book, *Gita Rahasya*, is considered by all Sanskrit scholars and Brahmin authorities as the best commentary on the *Gita*. Gandhi, being not a Brahmin, cannot be accepted as an authority on the *Gita* which is given the status of a *Veda*.

Hinduism sanctions violence: In the *Gita Rahasya*, Tilak makes it clear that both the *vedic* religion and Manu, the Hindu law-giver, sanction killing (violence).Both also suggest speaking of falsehood, says Gosavi. Tilak held that Krishna, the great Hindu god, sanctioned killing and as such violence is part of Hinduism. So, Gosavi criticises Gandhi for misinterpreting Hinduism. "Gandhi formulated no scientfic system of his philosophy" (Ibid p.11).

How then the very same Brahmins hailed Gandhi and described his teachings as a philosophy, renaming it as gandhism?

The answer to this question lies in the fact that this is the handiwork of "Socialist Brhamins" and not the honest "Sacred Brahmins".

Tilak's warning to Gandhi: Tilak was the first *vaidik* leader who launched the Hindu revivalist movement and Veer Savarkar, also a Chitpavan Brahmin and a founder of the RSS, was a disciple of Tilak. And it was Tilak who resented the growing popularity of Gandhi, a Gujarati Baniya (trading caste), and asked the "nationalists" to stop the passing of the leadership of the Indian "nationalist movement" from Brahmins into the hands of a non-Brahmin. Their fear was that if the non-Brahmin leadership gets strengthened under the influence of Gandhi, all that the *vaidiks* did to secure freedom for India by driving out the British will go waste. The *vaidik* efforts for freedom movement were aimed at replacing the British rule with a Brahmin rule. They feared that if Gandhi was allowed to grow too tall, he might come in the way of the Brahmin rule.

This was the secret of the Brahmin hatred of Gandhi and his ultimate murder. Richard Attenborough who produced the *Gandhi* film had no courage to say this because the film was financed by another Brahmin, Indira Gandhi, and intended to glorify the Brahmin contribution to India's freedom struggle.

Is it not clear that despite years of serving Brahmins, singing praise of the *Gita*, reciting the *Ramdhan*, campaigning against cow slaughter - which hit the stomach of the Muslims, Dalits and Tribals and Christians to whom beef is the cheapest food - attacking and criticising the Christians for converting the Dalits, the "Sacred Brahmins" still hated him and finally shot him dead?

RSS distributes sweets: Even when he was alive, Gandhi was India's forgotten man. He could use his weapon of *satyagraha* only against the British but not against the Brahmins. When he fasted against the British, the Brahmins liked it but when he fasted against the division of India, the "Socialist Brahmins" resented it. They came near the Birla House in Delhi shouting: "Let Gandhi die". Gandhi finally gave them what they wanted - Brahmin imperialism. They were happy that their objective was fulfilled. Their job was over. So he must go.

Gandhi's whole life was a waste. When the Hindu nazis were crying for their *mahatma*'s blood inside India and the *chaddi* boys distributed sweets in their *shakas* on his death, thousands of Muslims in Pakistan prayed in their mosques for the dying *mahatma*.

Savarkar and Golwalkar detested everything that Gandhi stood for and declared Gandhi as anti-Hindu, even anti-national. If "Socialist Brahmins" led by Jawaharlal Nehru had accepted his leadership it was because they wanted to exploit the *mahatma* to the maximum extent. The Brahmins have no permanent party. They have only permanent interests. This is true even to this day. That is why they never put all their eggs in one basket. They get distributed in different parties including the "communist" parties.

Muslim killed Gandhi?: The RSS, which had advance information about the Gandhi murder (Jan.30, 1948) distributed sweets all over India within minutes of his assassination but the enraged people set fire to some Chitpavan Brahmin houses in Maharashtra and Karnataka. The actual plan of the RSS was said to be to put the blame on Muslims for the Gandhi murder and in many parts of India, RSS had launched attacks on Muslim shops and houses. Reports said all plans were made to implicate Muslims in the Gandhi murder. It was a beautiful conspiracy. Godse had tattooed a Muslim name on his right arm and had undergone circumcision so that when he was caught by the police, he should be mistaken to be a Muslim, the reports said. Of course the *chaddi* boys, experts at rumour-mongering, were there waiting for the Godse shooting to spread the word that the fellow who shot Gandhi was a diehard Muslim. The conspiracy worked for sometime and did play havoc because on hearing the rumour that a Muslim killed Gandhi, the nazis had already started attacking Muslims in different cities.

Intelligence sources had definite information about Gandhi murder. Vallabhai Patel, then Union Home Minister, and Morarji Desai, then Home Minister in the erstwhile Bombay Government, also had advance information about the murder. Gandhi was a bone in the throat of Brahmins. Having taken control of India from the British, the *vaidiks* were worried that Gandhi might come in their way of imposing the brahminical imperialism. Hence they wanted to finish him as he was a nuisance.

Intellectual dishonesty: When the true history of India is going to be written by honest historians the role played by these people will get a proper treatment. The oppressed community has not yet produced outstanding scholars because the cream of the community has gone over to government services due to the job reservation in services. But soon Dalits will produce such scholars who will write a true history of India portraying the havoc played by brahminical imperialism and the part played by Gandhi to encourage it.

As of today, India has hardly any who can be called as an honest scholar. Because all the "scholars" of today are from the Aryan upper castes and their loyalty being to their caste *(jati)*, they can be hardly expected to speak out the truth. To speak out the truth, intellectual honesty is needed and this commodity is a rarity in India. That is why India has turned into a vast intellectual Sahara. If India has become a beggar nation today, sick man of the world, the blame entirely goes to the crowd of dishonest intellectuals who are crowding our academic world and journalistic empire. Dalits will break this tightly sealed fortress and set fire to their dung heap.

As over 85% of the India's Bahujan Samaj - the original inhabitants of India - is not having a media, it has not been possible to bring out the truth on Gandhi's murder and how the *vaidik* vampire wanted to put the blame on the Muslims for the murder.

Periyar saves Muslims: In some parts of Tamil Nadu, anti-Muslim riots had begun and panic-stricken Muslims rushed to Periyar E.V. Ramaswamy, the greatest Tamil leader of the non-Brahmin movement, requesting him to save Muslims. Dravida Kazhagam sources said heeding the Muslim SOS, Periyar rushed to the All India Radio station in Madras and announced that Gandhi was killed not by a Muslim but actually by a Brahmin. It was only after his appeal the anti-Muslim riots came to a stop.

In Bombay, mobs attacked Savarkar's residence and all over India RSS offices were attacked. Gandhi, the "Father of the Nation" and considered by a section of Indians as the greatest man of the 20th century, was murdered by a Brahmin. But except for some minor attacks on (RSS) *shakas* (units) and a few Chitpavan Brahmin houses, there was no other violence on Brahmins anywhere in India. No Brahmin was then killed as a revenge.

Sikh massacre in Delhi: But see the contrast. When Indira Gandhi, who never held any place in the heart of an Indian, was murdered (1985) allegedly by a Sikh, the very Hindus went on a killing spree in Delhi and many parts of North India. In Delhi alone, over 5,000 Sikhs were massacred. For these very same Hindus, Gandhi's life was not important because he was no Brahmin. But Mrs Gandhi was a Brahmin - a Kashmiri Brahmin. [*Dalit Voice.* Dec. 16, 1984: "*Why Beant Singh killed Indira Gandhi?*" in which we have compared the three famous killings :(1) Hindu god Krishna telling Arjuna to kill in the *Gita,* (2) Godse's killing of Gandhi and (3) Beant Singh killing Indira Gandhi].

Whatever it is, even to this day RSS has to live with the stigma of Gandhi murder despite an obliging court holding Godse not belonging to RSS but the Hindu Mahasabha. The RSS quickly disowned Godse. But the fact is that the RSS does not keep a record of its members' list. Even if the RSS claim is true, what is the material difference between the RSS and Hindu Mahasabha except between Tweedledee and Tweedledum? Be that as it may, the very fact that the RSS celebrated Gandhi's murder by distributing sweets proves its happiness over his assassination. Intellectual honesty needed a frank admission of the fact but that is a commodity rare with the *vaidiks*.

Sex perversion: The No.2 accused in the Gandhi murder case was Narayan Apte, described as a lecherous Brahmin teacher. (As regards sex perversion is concerned, Godse was equally an expert. Read *Nine Hours to Rama,* Stanley Wolpert, 1962, Hamish Hemilton, London). Savarkar was acquitted and died in 1966. Godse and Apte were hanged at Ambala Jail on Nov. 15, 1949. Justice Achhru Ram of the Punjab High Court, who heard Godse's appeal, said, "Godse personally argued his case". He paid tributes to Godse's mastery of facts. Apte and Godse had carried with them, when they started from Poona, a copy of the *Gita*, a sacred scripture of the Hindus, a map of the undivided India (a goal which the *vaidik* vampire has since given up) and a saffron flag of the RSS. Look at their devotion to brahminism. To them brahminism is more important than the country, because as Aryans and invaders the country does not belong to them.

Nathuram Godse died instantly. But Apte took a couple of minutes. Before they went to the gallows they shouted RSS slogans. To save brahminism, they do not mind sacrificing their lives. This is the true nazi style. And that is why as an honest Brahmin, whom we describe as "Sacred Brahmins" , we like Godse. But, alas, his tribe is becoming a rarity - crushed by the corrupt "Socialist Brahmins".

The introduction to the Godse book says Gandhi was fooling the public. Yes, he was. We agree with this charge. "When people go to the Raj Ghat to pay homage to Gandhi and repeat the vow of abiding by truth and non-violence, the writer feels that there is ever-lasting field in our country to befool the public", says the introduction. Gandhi symbolised the Hindu hypocrisy for which this country is so famous. Gandhi fooled the Dalits and other persecuted nationalities denied human rights. So much so, the Indian revolution got delayed by 50 years. Thanks to Gandhi.

Hambug of non-violence: But why did the RSS change its stand on Gandhi? RSS leaders, who were so honest during Golwalkar's regime, later started speaking lies. If today anybody criticises Gandhi, Hindu nazi fellows will be the first to pounce on such critics like a mad dog. (DV Editorial Feb. 16, 1997: *"Why all those who killed Gandhi bark at those criticising Gandhi?"* - see annexure). What else to conclude from the RSS leaders praising Gandhi now? The RSS leaders openly criticised Gandhi for preaching "non-violence" and they fought him on this. Savarkar had clearly declared that non-violence was never a part of

Hinduism, ridiculing Gandhi's *ahimsa* thereby *Dalit Voice* of June 1, 1993. [p.19] reproduced a document from Savarkar's book, *Hindurashtra Darpan* (1992, Veer Savarkar Prakashan, 40/1175, Nehru Nagar, Kurla East, Bombay - 24). Tilak, Savarkar, and Godse said Gandhi's humbug of non-violence made the Hindus cowards and they openly advocated violence as recommended by the Hindu "sacred scriptures". According to these interpreters of Hinduism their religion never abhorred violence.Every Hindu god practised violence. Look at their photos or images of Hindu gods posing with all types of deadly weapons. So, Godse was right and Gandhi wrong.

When the Hindu army marched into the Golden Temple (1984) and killed over 10,000 Sikhs including children and women, no Hindu leader protested. No Hindu leader has so far criticised the mass killing of Muslims. Amnesty International has described India as the world's most violent country. This description is perfectly right.

II - HINDUISM & VIOLENCE

The RSS in true Hindu spirit has always advocated and practised violence. In the 1983 Nellie (Assam) massacre of thousands of Muslims, the RSS was indicted by many Hindus themselves. In all RSS processions they carry lathies, sticks, swords and knives. RSS often indulges in violence and this is evident from the series of anti-Muslim, anti-Christian, anti-Dalit and anti-Sikh riots in different parts of the country. The police have found RSS offices packed with arms. Therefore, Godse has to be rightly congratulated for boldly admitting the truth that Hinduism stands for violence and not non-violence. Gandhi tried to hoodwink the world. Foreigners often deceived by the much-publicised "Hindu non-violence" and "tolerance" should take note of this.

***Ahimsa* made Hindu cowards:** In the part-I of Godse's book, answering the chargesheet he frankly admits that he practised violence, possessed a pistol, and says that he represented a Hindu fundamentalist school of thought (RSS) that always opposed the ideology of Gandhi:

> "I believe that the teachings of absolute *ahimsa* as advanced by Gandhi would ultimately result in emasculation of the Hindu community and thus make the community incapable of resisting the aggression or inroads of other communities especially the Muslims". (*May It Please Your Honour*, p. 7).

This sentence is an honest confession that Hindus or Hinduism stand for violence. In the *Gita*, the Hindu god, Krishna, also advocates violence. How then some people mistake that Hinduism stands for non-violence?

Gandhi was perhaps 20th century's most cunning and crafty fox in a saint's garb. But for him Hinduism (the popular name for brahminism) would have been dead even as the British left India. So, the credit for saving Hinduism and transferring the country from British imperialists to the more dangerous brahminical imperialists goes to Gandhi.

Though the non-violence aspect of it was smuggled into Hinduism by the *vaidiks,* borrowing it from Jainism to save brahminism from the jaws of Jainism and Budhism, which threatened the very survival of brahminism at the time of the Adi Sankara, no Hindu leader had raised this concept of non-violence to such a pre-eminent pedestal as Gandhi did. It was Gandhi who gave prestige to Hinduism and was responsible for making the whole world believe that the Hindus were the most non-violent people on earth. Therefore, those interested in knowing the facts of history will be surprised to learn that when Gandhi advertised the "Hindu non-violence", he was borrowing this concept from Jainism. Not even Budhism. Non-violence is alien to Hinduism. Godse, who is revered even now by every "Sacred Brahmin", has made this point clear when he killed Gandhi. According to him, non-violence is the weapon of the weak and the coward and Gandhi made the Hindus impotent.

Budhism & Ahimsa: Babasaheb Ambedkar devotes a section itself, "True meaning of *Ahimsa*", in his book, *Buddha and His Dhamma* (*Dr. Babasaheb Ambedkar Writings & Speeches*, Vol.11, Maharashtra Govt., Bombay, 1992, p.346). Babasaheb says Budha nowhere specifically refers to *Ahimasa* (non-violence). Despite this brahminical writers, in their bid to denigrate Budhism and keep the meat-eating over 90% of India's people out of Budhism, have successfully put out the falsehood that if one becomes a Budhist he must become a vegetarian as Budhism does not sanction violence. Babasaheb makes this point clear and says that Budha had no objection to meat-eating. Even Budhist monks can eat it if it is part of the alms given to them. *Ahimsa param dharma* is a Jain doctrine. It is not a Budhist principle. Babasaheb also says that Budha makes a difference between the "need to kill and the will to kill":

> "Budha did not ban killing where there was a need to kill. What he banned was killing where there was nothing but the will to kill". (p.346).

Babasaheb says:

> "Brahminism has in it the will to kill. Jainism has in it the will never to kill. Budha did not make *Ahimsa* a matter

of Rule... He enunciated it as a matter of Principle or way of life". (p. 347)

From this it is clear that the *vaidik* intention to link *ahimsa* with Budhism is to see that the meat-eating Bahujans (90% of India's population) do not take to Budhism.

We have the additional proof that Gandhi smuggled non-violence into Hinduism from another Brahmin and also a great supporter of the Hindu nazi philosophy. A Hindu nazi journalist, Arun Shourie, in the last chapter, "Gandhi and Tradition", of his book, *Hinduism - Essence and Consequence* (1979-Vikas), is all praise for Gandhi for giving a new interpretation to Hinduism. Gandhi, he says, quoting from Gandhi's journal, *Harijan*, questioned the *Manusmriti* which lays the entire ground rules for Hinduism. (Ibid p. 377). Gandhi called for a new edition of the sacred scriptures. "I would reject all scriptural authority if it is in conflict with sober reasons or the dictates of the heart". (Ibid p. 377). Who gave the authority to a non-Brahmin to question the authority of the "Sacred Brahmins"? But that is a separate subject.

Shot dead like a street dog: Gandhi tried to use a thorn to remove another thorn. In other words, he wanted to use the Brahmins by buttering the Brahmins. But the Brahmins proved more cunning than the Porbander Bania. Finally, it was the Brahmins who used him. Gandhi failed to shake even a hair of the Brahmins. Rather, the Brahmins milked him dry. Not only they milked him dry, rejected everything that he said, but finally shot him dead like a street dog. This is usual with brahminism.

Gandhi, therefore, became history's most magnificent failure.

Entire Bania community lifted up: Gandhi might have failed to boss over the Brahmins but he certainly secured their blessings to lift his Bania (Vaishya) community, ranking third in the caste hierarchy after the Brahmins and Kshatriyas. Until Gandhi came on the scene the Vaishyas were one of the most despised *jatis* - born out of *papayoni* (sinful vagina). They were treated like the *shudras*-though belonging to the twice-born (*dwija*) category.

The credit for uplifting the Bania community, particularly in the Western India and that too the Hindu Vaishyas but not the Jain (Marwadi Banias), goes entirely to this cunning Gujarati Bania. The Birlas, who rank No.2 among India's business houses, entirely owe their prosperity to Gandhi because it was Ghanashyam Das (G.D.) Birla, a Marwadi, who made the best use of Gandhi and also Kamalanayan Bajaj. Gandhi always stayed in the house of Birlas and finally died in Birla Bhavan. Kamalanayan Bajaj set up a sugar factory in UP as early as 1931. On the advice of Gandhi, he took over Mukand Iron Works. (*Asian Age* May 5, 1997).

The beauty of the *vaidik* philosophy is that it will not allow anybody to challenge its authority and lordship. With this one exception it will permit any other adjustment. Gandhi was allowed to lift his entire community (much smaller in population compared to Brahmins) up and amass wealth through exploitation. Today, the Hindu nazi *Brahamana Jati Party* (BJP) is considered a Brahmin-Bania party. The Brahmins run the party with the Bania money. The Banias have been allowed to amass wealth on the condition that they will be the loyal servants of Brahmins. Until Gandhi came on the scene, the Banias were ordinary people and in the past 50 years since independence (1947) they have come to the top position controlling the country's entire business world and also the media - but both kept at the disposal of Brahmins. Banias are behind most of the nazi-oriented violent eruptions in the country. All this is the result of Gandhi's efforts to make his *jati* as the servants of Brahmins - thereby losing the very identity of the *jati*.

Sanctimonious humbug: What is the test of a philosophy? The test is it should have social roots which will help transform a society and elevate its people. Did the "gandhian philosophy", whatever it may mean, transform India? Gandhi's "chief disciple", Jawaharlal Nehru, a Kashmiri Brahmin whom he groomed as India's first Prime

Minister, was not only Gandhi's bitterest critic but according to Nehru's biographer he was notorious for his drinking, womanising and love for good things of life, which are exactly opposite of what Gandhi is supposed to have stood for. Gandhism was buried fathoms deep even when Gandhi was alive. The people too rejected his "philosophy" if it can be called a philosophy. They rejected it because it assured them nothing. Gandhism became the other name for sanctimonious humbug. Gandhism is in fact the other name for Hinduism.

Gandhi tried the impossible in making a black crow into white. He wanted to bring about changes in brahminism not by fighting Brahmins but by buttering them, bum-licking them. Instead of launching an uncompromising war against brahminism, he thought he could win over the Brahmins and make them agree to change their value system. He tried to build a new superstructure without destroying the base.

Arun Shourie pays high tributes to Gandhi for trying to hold reason above Brahmin scriptures and says gandhism is the panacea for India's ills. But the same Arun Shourie who in this book is acting as the salesman for gandhism later joined the company of the very killers of Gandhi and became their salesman also.

Boneless wonder: And what is intriguing is that Gandhi is quoted by the thief, policeman, prosecuter, jailor, judge and the hangman. How can Gandhi be the hero for all? How can a particular person be the darling for all sections - exploiter and the exploited? This is the wonder of all wonders of gandhism - boneless wonder. Every political party in India, from the left extreme to the right extreme, publicly worships Gandhi and swears by gandhism. How is this possible? Even the communist parties are Gandhi admirers. That means Gandhi can be used by the devil as well as the angel. Gandhi can be interpreted any way you like.

Is there any person and his philosophy which can be equated to Gandhi and gandhism? We can understand the exploiters, who invariably are the upper caste Aryans, worshipping Gandhi. But the victims of upper castes, like Muslims, Christians, Sikhs and even some Dalits, worship Gandhi. The only person who challenged Gandhi, even when the *mahatma* was alive, was Dr. Babasaheb Ambedkar.

Cap that fits every head: Godse says he killed Gandhi for supporting Muslims but within ten years of writing his book in which he placed Gandhi next only to Budha, Arun Shourie, like a true Brahmin, defends the killing of thousands of Muslims in Assam. Like the devil quoting the scriptures, Brahmins quote Gandhi whenever it is convenient to them. We have any number of intellectual prostitutes like this in India. These intellectual prostitutes make money by selling gandhism and also get "national" awards and rewards. The very same fellows also make money by denigrating gandhism. And for attacking Gandhi also they get "national awards". The award- giver, and the award-taker, and those who write in praise of the award-winner, all belong to the same *jati*. This is the greatness of Gandhi and the Gandhi Cap which fits any and every head. These *vaidiks* have been fooling not only Indians but the whole world like this for centuries.

Gandhi is said to have tried to give a "new interpretation" to the *Gita* and this served the "Socialist Brahmins" very well to fool the *shudras* and use these unthinking people against the British as cannon-fodder. Dr. Babasaheb Ambedkar was the only person who was bold enough to stand up against Gandhi and expose him right during the very life time of the *mahatma*. But the media and the books being in the hands of Brahmins, what Babasaheb said could not percolate to the mass - except in places where he directly spoke to the people.

Enslavement of Dalits: The "new interpretation" given by Gandhi to the *Gita* was, however, not acceptable to the "Sacred Brahmins", who had manufactured the *Gita*. And that means Gandhi's interpretation of the *Gita* was unauthorised. Shourie may say that he ranks Gandhi next only to the Budha (Ibid p.388) but we have not heard of any "Sacred Brahmin" saying so.

Arun Shourie says that to Gandhi the "struggle" to liberate the slaves from suffering is the best way to realise the self. But we have not come across any such "struggle" that Gandhi led to liberate the "slaves". In India, the slaves are none other than the Untouchables whose undisputed leader, Babasaheb Ambedkar, called him the Enemy No.1 of the Untouchables. If Gandhi had actually helped liberation of the slaves, the slaves should have admitted it. But no slave has said that Gandhi played the part of a liberator. Babasaheb has cited any number of cases of Gandhi working against the interests of these slaves. (*What Congress and Gandhi have done to Untouchables* Vol. 9: *Babasaheb Ambedkar Writings & Speeches*, 1990).

BSO discards Gandhi: That Gandhi "fought" untouchability is yet another Hindu propaganda. His much-publicised "Epic Fast" (Pyarelal: *The Epic Fast*, 1984, Akhil Bharat Anusuchita Jati Parishad, 74-South Avenue, New Delhi-110 001) of 1932, which ended in the disasterous "Poona Pact", was not a fast intended for the removal of untouchability but to keep the Untouchables as the slaves of Hindus. Gandhi deceived the Untouchables, the sudras, the Muslims, Sikhs, or the entirc mass of Indians (Bahujan Samaj) and bound them head and foot and threw them to the wolves. The Bahujans being mostly poor and illiterate might not have realised this mischief but that does not hide the fact that he did not deceive them. On the other hand, he spent his whole life trying to rescue brahminism before being trampled upon by the victims of brahminism.

The ruling Brahminical Social Order of India, comprising 15% of the Aryans, became rulers after driving out the British solely because of Gandhi and gandhism. That the members of the BSO except paying lip sympathy to their "Father of the Nation" have completely discarded and forgotten Gandhi is a different subject. BSO keeps his portrait only in govt. offices but not in their houses. Gandhi ideally suits the rulers to cover up their double-speak, hypocrisy. Brahmins, who got the maximum benefit out of Gandhi by becoming the rulers of India, did not have the gratefulness to denounce Godse, the killer of Gandhi.

It is to rescue Brahmins and install them as the rulers of India that Gandhi took all the pains to pacify the angry sudras and Dalits by "misinterpreting" the Brahmin scripture (*Gita According to Gandhi* - Mahadev Desai, Navajivan, Ahmedabad - 1956 reprint). The Brahmins liked his "misinterpretation" because it suited them. To them, he was a good joker. His jokes entertained the masses, hoodwinked them, made them better slaves of the upper castes.

A counter-revolutionary: Arun Shourie says "Gandhi would still be the most original social thinker that we have had since the Buddha". (Ibid p. 399). What is the "original" social philosophy that Gandhi left us? He defended brahminism and its caste system; and right from the days of the Budha up to Babasaheb, every fight of the revolutionaries was against these two things. That means he was not an "original social thinker", but a counter-revolutionary.

The difference between Gandhi and Godse was that the former was a dangerous "Socialist Brahmin" , a concealed enemy and the latter was a "Sacred Brahmin", an open enemy. The latter advocated the use of violence to suppress the masses but Gandhi advocated non-violence to do the same job in a subtle way. Therefore, if Godse is our open enemy, Gandhi is our disguised enemy. Godse is an honest enemy but Gandhi a dishonest foe. Between the two, we prefer Godse and not Gandhi. He killed us with his "kindness". It was a kiss of death. That is why when in all other parts of the world the slaves are victims of violence, in India we slaves are the victims of non-violence.

Hindu Rashtra: Gandhi used religious idioms to mobilise the masses against the British and handed over the country to Brahmins and Banias. Tilak, Golwalkar and Godse could not have succeeded in this task. But Gandhi succeeded where the "Sacred Brahmins" failed. To that extent he was crafty, cunning and extremely deceptive. "Sacred Brahmin" theories, being antagonistic to the interests of slaves, they would react and violently revolt but Gandhi being a "Socialist Brahmin" misinterpreted the brahminical theories to deceive the slaves and thereby gave them slow poison. If brhaminism is the reigning religion of India today, the credit goes to Gandhi and not to the RSS-BJP pure *vaidik* parties. It was Gandhi who converted India into a *Hindu Rashtra* and not the RSS-BJP. That means those who want to destroy brahminism need not fight the RSS-BJP Hindu nazis. Their Enemy No. 1 is Gandhi and gandhism which have to be buried 100 fathoms deep. That is why the Bahujan Samaj Party leaders, Kanshi Ram and Mayawati, chose to attack Gandhi but had political alliance with BJP in Uttar Pradesh.

Humbug of trusteeship theory: Gandhi's "trusteeship theory" is one such beautiful weapon to fool the people. This theory was later advocated by the Sarkari Sant, Vinoba Bhave, and the Bihari Kayasth, Jayaprakash Narayan, to perpetuate exploitation. Not one capitalist including the Birlas, the biggest beneficiaries of this gandhian theory, has been able to transcend their class interests. They all used the trusteeship theory to further enrich themselves.

His another weapon to fool the masses and the world outside was non-violence. The state uses violence against the people even as it swears by gandhian non-violence. Every police station has a picture of Gandhi at the very entrance. Those who shout loudest about non-violence are those who in fact are the most violent persons in India. Morarji Desai, a Nagar Brahmin from Gandhi's own Gujarat and a former Prime Minister of India, was notorious for his use of violence. So also another Prime Minister, Indira Gandhi, who sent the Hindu Army to butcher over 10,000 Sikhs inside the Golden Temple in 1984. P.V. Narasimha Rao, the Neogi Brahmin who is called the living *Chanakya*, conspired in the destruction of Babri Masjid causing the death of thousands of Muslims - all in the name of Gandhi and gandhism. Every killing done by our rulers was done in the name of Gandhi. Non-violence for the slaves and violence for the rulers. The rulers are very particular that masses should practice non-violence because they are afraid that mob violence may butcher them wholesale.

The RSS and Godse considered Gandhi as pro-Muslim. But to the Muslims, Gandhi was rabidly anti-Muslim and M.A. Jinnah, the greatest Muslim leader of India, called him a Hindu leader. So also Dr B.R. Ambedkar. Hence Dalits led by Dr Ambedkar were not alone in considering Gandhi as their enemy. That means the "Sacred Brahmins" on the one side and the non-Muslims like Dalits, Christians and Sikhs (considered non-Hindus) also declared Gandhi hostile to their cause but what a pity that even the very custodians of Hinduism declared him as their enemy. Even after doing so much of service to Hinduism, the Brahmins refused to recognise his services to Hinduism. Is it not clear from this that the Brahmins would recognise none else as their leader except a Brahmin?

Godse, who had earlier failed to kill Gandhi after an abortive attempt in the Birla House, says he bought a pistol from a refugee as he was moving around the refugee camps in Delhi. Referring to his relationship with Savarkar, he says (*May it Please Your Honour*, p. 14) Savarkar was "born in a devotional Brahmin family". He also admits that for several years he was in the RSS. He says Savarkar gave him Rs. 15,000 at that time to start a daily paper. What is Rs. 15,000 worth today? How rich Savarkar might have been? Money was no problem to Gandhi-killers. They took a plane from Bombay to Delhi - and led a luxurious life. Big money was involved in the killing of Gandhi and the state machinery knew all this and yet kept silent.

Godse's sole aim in life was to "teach" a lesson to Gandhi and to prove to the world that the "Hindu too could be intolerant when his honour was insulted". (Ibid p.19).

The Hindu is noted for his intolerance. So famous a writer like V.S. Naipaul complains that though he was an Indian and born a Hindu Brahmin, his writings were not so far translated to any Indian language because he was critical of the Hindus. The Hindu would never tolerate any criticism. He resents truth. Therefore, Godse is not right. There is no need to "insult" the Hindu to make him intolerant. Those who want to know more about the Hindu intolerance may read the French missionary, the Abbe

Dubois' book on India, *The Hindu Customs and Manners*, Indian Educational Services, C-2/15-SDA, P.B.No. 4534, New Delhi-110016. The very basis of Hinduism is hatred. It hates Untouchables. It hates Muslims. It hates women. Manu, the Hindu law- giver, gives a long list of people whom a Hindu has to hate and destroy. "Blue Star Operation" (1984) against Sikhs, Babri Masjid (1992) against Muslims, the Kashmir War, the anti-Mandal war and violence - to mention only the most serious ones - are all products of the Hindu hatred. Hate produces more hate and as of today the whole India has become a hate-filled hot bed frying its persecuted nationalities denied human rights.

Tagore's national anthem praising British king: The RSS, the Hindu Mahasabha and like-minded Hindus have never recognised Aug. 15 as the "Independence Day". Godse says that on this day Savarkar always hoisted the RSS flag and not the national flag. Nor do the "Sacred Brahmins" recognise the national anthem, *Jana Gana Mana*, which Rabindranath Tagore composed in praise of the visiting British emperor, the King George the V (*Dalit Voice*, Sept. 1, 1985 p.8: "*Tagore sang national anthem in praise of British King?*"). Ashish Nandy, also a Bengali, dubbed Tagore as anti-national in his book, *The Illegitimacy of Nationalism*, Oxford University. (DV Oct. 1, 1994 p. 22: "*Tagore anti-national?*").

If a non-*vaidik* says the same thing it becomes an anti-national act punishable as treason. But if the Brahmins refuse to sing the national anthem, it will be described as a "patriotic act". We have two sets of laws in India - one for the upper castes and another for the masses. If a starving man out of poverty and hunger steals two chicken, he is called a thief, handcuffed, paraded and jailed. If you don't pay the tax amounting to millions of rupees, you get a national award. (*Dalit Voice*, Oct. 1, 1994 p.10: *"Two yardsticks: one for Phoolan Devi and another for Harshad Mehta")*. Phoolan Devi, a Backward Caste woman who is hailed as India's greatest woman human rights leader, was put in jail, tormented and tortured but Harshad Mehta, a Gujarati Bania of Gandhi's *jati*, is being invited by Rotary

Club, Lions Club, Donkeys Club, Monkeys Club all over India. For cheating the Govt. of India, he is hailed as a great brainy, brilliant boy. This is the Hindu double-standard which Gandhi popularised.

Anti-Hindu Gandhi?: Godse goes on arguing that Gandhi was anti-Hindu but nowhere he gives any proof for his argument. To oppose Gandhi he decided to organise programmes on "secret and dictatorial" lines perfectly in tune with the nazi methods adopted by his party. Nazis do not believe in democracy. In the *Bunch of Thoughts*, Golwalkar makes it clear that democracy is unsuited to India and the RSS does not believe in democracy. Hinduism and democracy cannot co-exist.

Godse says he kept Savarkar informed of his activities but at the same time he asserts that Savarkar did not know his plans to kill Gandhi. The police records, however, prove that the conspiracy to kill Gandhi was hatched in the Bombay house of Savarkar on Jan. 14, 1948 (*Freedom at Midnight*, Vikas, 1976, p. 383-84).

When non-RSS leaders like Morarji Desai and Vallabhabhai Patel of the Congress Party could know it, how could an insider be ignorant? That means Godse deliberately bluffed to save Savarkar from the gallows. To a *vaidik* uttering falsehood is like uttering a *mantra*.

Even Brahmin leaders in the government and the police also did their best to save Savarkar. The Gandhi murder inquiry itself was stalled. The police did their best to stone-wall the probe. The RSS did its best to escape responsibility and the willing judges obliged it. The whole thing was a farce.

Coming back to the subject of violence, Godse makes out a perfect case in favour of it. To prove his point he quotes from the Hindu scriptures, the *puranas*, epics, and the different acts of violence committed by the Hindu gods. His point is that the brahminical philosophy always stood for violence. According to him Gandhi was a crook in calling Shivaji, Rana Pratap Singh and Guru Gobind Singh as misguided patriots. (Dr. M.M. Kothari: *Critique of Gandhi*,

1997, Critique Publications, 5-Umed Hospital Rd., Jodhpur - 342 003).

Sikhs hate Gandhi: Even the militant Sikh leader, Sant Bhindranwale, had attacked Gandhi for criticising Guru Gobind Singh and said in an interview to the *Sunday* (May 15, 1986) that Sikhs would not recognise Gandhi as the "Father of the Nation". In the whole of Punjab, there is no statue of Gandhi except an ugly one at Batala. And this particular statue is always guarded by the police, for Sikhs often put garlands of slippers round its neck.

Hinduism is, therefore, very intolerant in matters that affect the Brahminical Social Order. It will tolerate only those who bow and prostrate before the Brahmin. Protestors shall be liquidated in the name of God. Look at the *Gita*. It preaches hatred against materialists. It calls them demons. (Arun Shourie: *Hinduism*-Vikas-p. 362).

III - "SOCIALIST BRAHMINS" vs THE "SACRED BRAHMINS"

What has been going on in India is nothing but a "fight" between two sections of Brahmins - "Sacred Brahmins" or those described as reactionary, communal, orthodox, nazi-minded upper castes led by the Sankaracharies on one side and the "Socialist Brahmins", being described as progressive, marxist upper castes like M.K. Gandhi, Mrs. Indira Gandhi, E.M.S. Namboodiripad etc. on the other side. This mock fight-a sort of a shadow boxing - between these two sections is given the colour as if it is a great ideological battle between the "reactionaries" and the "progressives". Different "socialist" and "communist" parties and other appendages are manufactured to fool the gullible masses. The leaders of both the sections - socialist camp and the Hindu nazi camp - are upper castes only. Both the sections of Aryans are united in keeping the *shudras* and Dalits in their places. They think alike in keeping the existing Brahminical Social Order as it is. They are also one in maintaining that Brahmins alone shall rule. They may not say so in so many words but their actions amount to that. Godse's argument (ibid, p. 30) confirms this interpretation:

> "The clique which has got into power with the patronage of the British... is now trying to exploit Gandhi's death... for its selfish aims. But the history will give them their proper place in the niche of fame."

Dialogue of Bhoodevatas: By this "clique", Godse was referring to Jawaharlal Nehru, a Kashmiri Brahmin and the father of Mrs. Indira Gandhi. Nehru was equally notorious for his brahminism. As regards keeping India under the Brahmin rule, he had no difference of opinion with the RSS. The difference between the "Socialist Brahmins" and the "Sacred Brahmins" is not ideological. Both the groups just put on a show of fighting in public. This is just to fool the Bahujan masses. But both the groups are united in keeping India under the Brahmin hegemony. One is complementary to the other. Like one stone rubbing the other and producing sparks, the "Socialist Brahmins" rub the "Sacred Brahmins" and vice versa and together produce electricity. The one wants the other because it is the "Sacred Brahmins" who always help the "Socialist Brahmins" to remain in power. The Congress, a party of "Socialist Brahmins", has been in power only because of the Hindu nazi party led by the "Sacred Brahmins." (For a further development of this theory of "Sacred Brahmins versus Socialist Brahmins" read our book, *Dialogue of the Bhoodevatas*, Dalit Sahitya Akademy, 1993).

The "Socialist Brahmins" led by Nehru were bent upon the partition of India because by this they could drive out a vocal section of North Indian Muslims into a separate country and to that extent their job would become easier to ride rough shod over the Bahujans. Subsequent events have proved that Nehru and the "Socialist Brahmins" were right and the "Sacred Brahmins" wrong. The British rule was replaced by a more tyrannical Brahmin rule and the oppression of the Dalits and the *sudras* reached intolerable limits. Brahmin imperialism has since reached its dizzy heights. (*Hindu Imperialism* by Swami Dharma Thirtha, Dalit Educational Literature Centre 1941, PO.Box. 2296, Madras - 600 023:) .

Gandhi corrupted Brahmins: Gandhi, though a *vaishya* belonging to the third-grade of the *varnashram dharma*, is described as a "Socialist Brahmin", despite not being a Brahmin. Until this wily Gujarati Bania came on the scene, this country had not seen a deceptive "Socialist Brahmin" like Gandhi. The Brahmins as *vaidiks* confined themselves to their daily rituals, temple-going, eating, their study and allied activities. As they had their own exclusive, secluded dwelling places, they confined themselves to their houses, temples and *agraharas*. And even while going to temples they used to maintain the distance from the rest, fearing pollution. Brahmins all over India were by and large a harmless lot. They hardly took any interest in the affairs outside their closed *vaidik* circles. Neither they used to interfere with the non-*vaidik* people nor the others tried to meddle with the Brahmins. There was a wall between the two and the non-*vaidiks* seldom knew what was going on the other side of the wall. So much so, the Brahmins looked harmless.

Gandhi for the first time in the history of India tried to break this wall and goaded the Brahmins to "take interest in the *Harijans* to atone for the sin they committed against *Harijans.*" It was Gandhi who for the first time initiated the *Harijan* temple-entry drive, forcing the Brahmins to take the non-Hindu Untouchables into Hindu temples which do not belong to them. Nor have the Untouchables expressed any desire for temple entry. Gandhi forced the Brhamins to interfere with our society and thereby complicated the whole thing and consequently caused good lot of confusion in the society.

Curse of India: Gandhi inaugurated the era of "Socialist Brahmins" who have become a curse on the Indian society. "Sacred Brahmins" are an honest people. They believe in their *varsnashrama dharma*, Aryan (foreign) origin, superior status, purity of blood, racism, enslavement of all *shudras* and *ati-shudras* including their own women. But the Gujarati Bania brought confusion and told a section of the gullible Brahmins waiting to grab political power on the exit of the British that "democracy" was coming to India in which only those who secured the majority votes could get elected. Since non-Brahmins and particularly the Untouchables were a huge chunk, they would be mightily pleased and vote wholesale to Brahmins if they won over the *Harijans* through certain gimmicks like temple-entry, inter-dining *Harijans* welfare and such tricks. He told them that since the *Harijans* were almost 100% illiterate, poor and destitutes, a little trick here and there would bring a ground-swell of goodwill among *Harijans* who, noted for their good-heart, gratefulness and sincerity, would fall flat before the Brahmins and elect them as leaders. This argument of Gandhi convinced some Brahmin leaders like Nehru, C. Rajagopalachari, etc., and created a battalion of "Socialist Brhamins" who caused all the confusion and the consequent chaos in the Indian politics. We have no quarrel with "Sacred Brahmins" like B.G. Tilak, Savarkar, Godse, Golwalkar, etc. They were honest Brahmins and we like honest Brhamins. Because they don't interfere with us and we don't interfere with them. Brahmins should take this as a warning and restore their purity and get back to their exclusivity.

That is why we like the *Brahmana Jati Party* (BJP) and call it by that name because it is a party of *vaidiks*, for *vaidiks* and by *vaidiks*. This Hindu nazi party is honest enough to declare that they don't recognise Gandhi as the "Father of Nation". When the Hindu nazi leader, A.B. Vajpayee, became the Prime Minister for just 14 days, he refused to visit Raj Ghat, Delhi, where Gandhi was cremated, as every PM does immediately after being sworn in. He was honest enough to say that he did not recognise Gandhi. V.P. Singh in his first address to the country as PM paid tributes only to Lohia and Jayaprakash Narayan. He did not mention Gandhi. The Hindu nazi party's mouthpiece, *Organiser* (Jan. 7, 1990) praised V.P. Singh for excluding Gandhi in his speech. (DV Feb. 1, 1990 p.20: "*Hindu nazis refuse to recognise Gandhi.*")

Brahminical imperialism: For the first time in Indian history, the Brahmins got the whole country to rule. Before the British and Muslim rule, at no time the Brahmins were in full control of the subcontinent. The Peshwas were ruling only a part of Western India. Gandhi handed over the whole of India (barring Pakistan) on a golden plate to Brahmins. (*Dalit Voice* Editorial, July 1, 1992: "*Brahminism is Enemy no. 1 for the whole world*" and "*Brahminism - Father of Fascism, Racism, Nazism*" - 1996 Dalit Sahitya Akademy).

To fight the Muslims and Christians, Godse commends the RSS resolution to "militarise the Hindus". Here we have a doubt. How can the Hindus get militarised? First of all, the 'Hindus' are not a martial race. The debacle suffered by the Hindus in their war against China is still green in our memory. The Indian army, described as the fourth largest in the world, got defeated in Sri Lanka at the hands of the Lankan Tamil Tigers' rag-tag 2,000-strong force of young boys and girls. Secondly, the Hindus cannot get themselves united as they are divided by the caste. The really militant people, the Dalits and Tribals, Muslims and

Sikhs are kept out of the military and disarmed. Sikhs, like the Muslims, have turned anti-Hindu. How then the "Hindus" can get militarised? Besides, the Hindus who are not even 15% of India's population are supposed to be vegetarians. Can vegetarians become a martial race? Can *idli-sambar* and grass-eating Brahmins and Banias face beef-eating Muslims? And even among Hindus not all are vegetarians. Even among Brahmins those from West Bengal, Kashmir, Himachal Pradesh and coastal Karnataka are meat-eaters.

RSS apology: During the Emergency, the so-called militancy of the RSS was proved to be a total hoax. RSS chief Balasaheb Deoras and hundreds of his *chaddi* boys gave written apologies to the government and said they would prostrate before Indira Gandhi if only they were released from jails. How could such a nation of cowards get militarised? Forget about their martial prowess, Hindus are not capable of building even an organisation. If there are three Hindus, they will have four ideas, says Dr. V.K.R.V. Rao, a Karnataka Brahmin, in his book *Swami Vivekananda: The Prophet of Vedantic Socialism* (quoted in *Sunday Standard* book review, Jan. 27, 1980 by Kapil Vatsayan).

Godse accuses Gandhi of divide and rule but how can anybody divide a set of people if they are not willing to be divided? The Hindu caste system has divided the Hindus on an ascending order of reverence and descending degree of contempt and that is why they are too willing to be divided. The Hindus will remain a house divided as long as the caste system is there. RSS leaders now and then express their fear that Hindus may be reduced to a minority in India. Their fear is genuine. When the Dalits and BCs realise their slavery under the Aryan invaders, the "Hindus" will be reduced to a minority. This is bound to happen soon. Already Dalits have declared they are not Hindus and never Hindus. So also the Sikhs. Jains have joined this list of non-Hindus. (DV March 1, 1997 p.22: "*Hindus admit Jains are not Hindus*"). Many more will say so soon. Backward Castes are fast realising this fact. The "Hindus" will soon become a minority and perhaps only Brahmins will remain to be called Hindus. And even they will not accept this name as it has a derogatory meaning.

Godse holds Gandhi responsible for dividing India. He says, "the existence of Gandhi should be brought to an end immediately" (Ibid, p.40). We agree with his statement that "Gandhi was guilty of blunder after blunder, failure after failure and disaster after disaster" (Ibid p. 41). Gandhi was indeed history's most magnificent failure. Gandhi's only success was that he put a stamp of respectability to Hindu humbugs parading with *khadi* and gandhi cap. (DV Guest Editorial by Dr. Velu Annamalai, July 16, 1994: "*US Dalits shatter myth of mahatma: A Document on Gandhi in his own words*").

❁ ❁ ❁ ❁

IV - A COUNTER-REVOLUTIONARY?

Did Gandhi play a counter-revolutionary role preventing a genuine revolution in India? Capitalists like G.D. Birla knew the crucial importance of this role of Gandhi, and, financed him. So too many other capitalists like Kamalanayan Bajaj etc.

An expert who has gone into this question of Gandhi linking profits with politics reveals the big business support the *mahatma* received. Pius Ganguly reviewing (*Statesman*, Sunday Magazine-Feb. 16, 1986) the book of Claude Markovits, *Indian Business and National Politics* (Cambridge University, Orient Longman, 1985), says:

> "The ascendancy of rightists and moderates within the Congress over the radical leftists during the late thirties also encouraged the industrialists to line up with the Congress. The re-establishment of Gandhian dominance over the Congress, confirmed by the resignation and ouster of Subhas Bose, suited the big business. Markovits suggests in the same vein that the Indian capitalists were invariably concerned at the Congress agitation over showing revolutionary potential. In fact capitalist support to the Congress became increasingly dependent on the nationalist party's ability to demonstrate that it could replace the British Raj as the guarantee of the existing order, in the urban areas as well as in the countryside. This was partly achieved during the period of the Congress Ministries in 1937-39 and it had a decisive impact on the political attitude of most Indian businessmen.
>
> "Pursuing the same line, the author argues that the rallying of the majority of Indian capitalists to the Congress in the countryside towards closer links with the landlords is a clear sign that the maintenance of the existing agrarian order, in spite of its many imperfections, suited them both politically and economically. The Indian capitalists, according to Markovits, were as much traders and financiers as industrialists and were not in principle committed to industrialization.
>
> "Driving his point further, Markovits contends that Indian businessmen appreciated strong bureaucratic rule and primarily wished to see a set of British bureaucrats replaced by a set of indigenous ones who would be more

open to capitalist influence. From 1937 it became increasingly evident that a future Congress Raj would not represent a complete break with the colonial state. Although incorporating democratic forms, it was to be basically a successor regime keeping the strong bureaucratic framework of its predecessor. This appears to have played an important role in influencing the political attitude of Indian business.

"Markovits' study yields the impression that the postures of the Indian big business vis-a-vis nationalist struggle were primarily determined by an awareness of its class interests. This, however, is not to deny the divergence in outlook among its individual members or groups. The author notes that the most modern section of Indian business, centered around the Tatas, was "the least pro-nationalist". On the other hand, G.D. Birla, Ambalal Sarabhai and Kasturbhai Lalbhai were always very close to Gandhiji and their interaction in the fields of nationalist politics and economy was highly significant", says Pius Ganguly.

Gujarati Banias financed British: V.T. Pavlov, a Russian author, in his book, *Historical Promises for India's Transition to Capitalism* (Nanka Publishing House, Moscow, 1978) explodes the myth that the upper castes of India led the struggle against the British. He proves that the Gujarati Banias, forefathers of M.K. Gandhi, were the greatest supporters of British colonialists (DV Dec. 1, 1994 p.22: "*Marwadis and Gujarati Banias financed British Rulers*").

Geoffery Moorhouse, a British author, in his, *India Brittanica* (Granada Publishing Ltd., 8-Grafton St., London, 1984) reveals how Gandhi crushed all them who he considered anti-British.

> "... The extremists had been gaining upper hand in Congress and Gandhi wanted none of them, if only because they might provoke the British into even uncompromising measures. Skilfully he isolated subhash Chandra Bose and drove him into a political wilderness..." (p.182).

Madhukar Kamble, (Dalit Voice May 1, 1996 p.23) says Gandhi made many compromises with the British. He shrewedly got rid of Subhas Chandra Bose. During the

Second World War, he was so moved by the British plight that he wanted to call of his "independence struggle".

M.N. Roy, a Bengali Brahmin and the founder of the communist movement in India, has said Gandhi actually worked to put down the stirrings of a popular revolt among the Indian masses. Samaren Roy in his book, *M.N. Roy and Mahatma Gandhi* (Minerva Publications, Calcutta, 1987), brings out this point. Gandhi joined hands with upper castes/class and did his best to nip any revolution in the bid (DV March 16, 1990: "*M.N.Roy said gandhism was nothing but fascism*").

Congress supported British: Upper caste writers have tried to paint a glorious picture of Gandhi and his Congress Party and created a mammoth myth of the *mahatma* to bamboozle us,frighten us. But history is a great leveller, road-roller that will bulldoze all such falsehoods. In the book, *India and The Raj, 1919-1947*, by Suniti Kumar Ghosh (Sabarnalekha, 1989, and his ealrier book, *The Indian Big Bourgeoisie: Its Genesis, Growth & Character*), pulls out the mask of the *mahatma* (DV March 1, 1990 p.14: *"Devastating Portrait of Gandhi: Congress supported British"*). We had written an Editorial itself: *"Did Gandhi fight the British and Big business?"* (DV, May 1, 1989) which is based on the book of Suniti Kumar Ghosh who exposed Gandhi's pathological connections with his *jatwala*, G.D. Birla, who took full advantage of the *mahatma*. During the first World War itself the Birlas became multi millionaires. (Ram Nivas Jaju: *G.D. Birla- A Biography*). The Birlas had never opposed the British rule. That is why long before the Muslim League demanded the partition of India, he (Birla) had pleaded for it-a fact historians are not aware of or ignore", says Ghosh (Indian Bourgeoisie and Imperialism, *Economic & Political Weekly*, Special Number. Nov. 1988 p.2445-58).

Gandhi was also close to Purushotam Thakurdas who along with G.D. Birla founded the Federation of Indian Chambers of Commerce and Industry. Frank Moraes in his biography, *Sir Purushottam Thakurdas*, says Congressmen themselves staged a demonstration before his palatial house in Bombay for supporting the British. Not only Gandhi but all his lieutenants including Nehru, Vallabhabhai Patel had close connections with the Indian capitalists who were pro-British, says Moraes quoting N.Mansergh, editor-in-chief of the book, *The Transfer of Power*, 1942, Vol. I. Fazlul Huq, a barrister from London and the author of the book *Gandhi: Saint or Sinner?* (Dalit Sahitya Akademy, 1991) in a long article: "*Did Gandhi oppose British Imperialism and Aparthied ?*" in the *Dalit Voice* (Jan. 16, 1990 p.21-23) also makes out the point that Gandhi from the beginning to the end was a stooge of the British. The Western and the Indian brahminical media created the illusion of sainthood around Gandhi and made people believe that he fought the aparthied in South Africa. All these make it clear that Gandhi was puttting on a show of fighting the British while secretly he was in league with the same people to see that his *jatwalas* take over India. All the upper castes, who are also the property-owners, and their media, covered up this counter-revolutionary character of Gandhi as they were sure that Gandhi was working for their caste-class interests.

Cow- slaughter ban hits Muslims: Gandhi's so-called love for Muslims, which Muslims themselves never felt as genuine, was more in the interest of gaining a cheap popularity and helping the ruling class-caste interests. If Gandhi had loved Muslims with what heart could he hit their stomach by harping on the ban on cow -slaughter?

He sought the Muslim support to fight the Dalits. Except saying that the Hindus and Muslims were brothers, he did nothing to cement this brotherhood. Not only he could not stop the division of India and Pakistan but even within India he could not stop the persecution of Muslims. And this persecution is increasing daily as years pass and gandhians are in the forefront of anti-Muslim riots.

As long as brahminism remains what it is, it will continue to regard Muslims and Christians as a separate nation. It is only by using the Muslims as a whipping boy it is possible for the Hindu nazis and the other Hindu warlords to mouth the "Hindu unity" slogans. On what other issues the RSS can unite the "Hindus" divided by castes except through its "hate-Muslim" mantra? The Hindu nazis, therefore, very much want the "Muslim problem" to continue so that it can go on pointing at this imaginary "enemy" to divert the attention of the slaves and thus go on lording over them and Dalits. This is the conspiracy behind all anti-Muslim riots. The *shudras* and the Dalits would never accept the Brahmin leadership and would even revolt against it. To prevent such a revolt, the Hindu nazis go on pointing to them an imaginary enemy so that the *vaidik* leadership over the masses remains in tact. We hope the Dalits and the *shudras* would see through this game and rip open the brahminical humbug.

Chinese revolution: If Gandhi had been really great and gandhism a philosophy of social change, why the oppressed Indian masses did not accept this philosophy? Soviet Russia and China also had their own *mahatmas*. Their philosophy of Leninism and Maoism were accepted and effectively implemented by their peoples. Both the countries had undergone a Revolution, and following that a thorough-going socio-economic reform had taken firm roots. The peoples in those countries had accepted them and proved it to the whole world that they were indeed benefitted by their respective philosophy of Leninism and Maoism. During our visit to China (1981) we were eye-witnesses to the miracle of Mao. A people or society accept a philosophy only when it is advantageous to them. Just as the people get the government they deserve, they also get the leader they deserve. The Chinese deserved Mao and the upper caste Hindus (Aryans) deserved Gandhi and his bogus gandhism. In what way gandhism helped India except as a cover for our traditional exploiters to suck more blood out of us? Gandhism became a convenient tool for the ruling class. Some of the economic aspects of gandhism may be good but the ruling class never refers to them because they are not in its interest.

Why people rejected gandhism: One common answer given by the ruling class is that "gandhism is no doubt good but what can we do if the people do not practise it?"

Our reply is that no oppressed people will ever reject what is good to them. Nowhere in history the people rejected a philosophy that promised them a better, happier life. The people found gandhism counter-revolutionary and hence rejected it. But India's ruling class embraced it because it badly wanted a counter-revolutionary philosophy in its own interest. Therefore, we cannot blame the people for rejecting gandhism.

The *Gandhi* film and many other stories going round tell us that Gandhi was opposed to partition. But the truth as told by Godse is different and we have historical evidence to believe that the Godse version is true:

> "In 1943 while Gandhi was on fast... and none allowed inside except the nearest and the dearest, C. Rajagopalachari (Rajaji) smuggled himself into Gandhi's room and hatched a plot of conceding Pakistan which Gandhi allowed him to negotiate with Jinnah". (p. 60 of Godse book).

Myth-making is a flourishing Indian industry. And Gandhi is one such myth - the guru of the carpet-baggers.

Rajaji, called the "Southern Fox" and an extraordinarily cunning Brahmin from Madras , was considered one of the first persons to grasp the significance of partition of India and its advantages to Brahmins. The "Sacred Brahmins" led by the RSS was honest enough to oppose the partition but the dishonest "Socialist Brahmins" led by Nehru and Rajaji thought that in an undivided "independent" India, it would be difficult for the Brahmins to check the rising aspirations of the "low caste" Bahujans. And when the "low caste" (proletariat) unrest gets uncontrollable they are certain to join with the Muslims and Christians, their co-sufferers, as both the sections are the victims of a common enemy. Dr. Babasaheb Ambedkar's famous book, *Pakistan or Partition of India*(1990 *Babasaheb Ambedkar Writings & Speeches*, Maharashtra Govt.) also appeared just then (1945) and they decided that unless the Muslims are driven out they would prove a greater danger to Brahmins inside. Brahmins forming less than 5% of the total population of India will not be able to control, much less thwart a revolution if the Dalits explode with the help of the enemies of Hinduism, namely Muslims, Christians and Sikhs. This fear was not imaginary but real and that is why the Brahminical Social Order takes any unity of the Dalits and Muslims seriously and deploys police and even army to put down any such effort towards unity.

Some Brahmins may become furious on reading this book. They may file cases, may call it defamatory, seditious anti-national. They may say that we are preaching hatred and trying to create disaffection between communities. They may also allege that we are inciting violence. But it must be noted that we have some Brahmins in India like M.N. Roy, D.D.Kosambi, Gore, Dr A.R. Desai, Justice V.R. Krishna Iyer, Justice Tarkunde who have risen above their caste interests. Therefore, the above words are addressed to only such of those Brahmins who may wear the cap if it fits them.

That is why we say "Socialist Brhamins" are more dangerous to us than the "Sacred Brahmins".

V - TRUTH ON PARTITION OF INDIA

The developments since the "partition" of India(1947) have made us realise the futility of forming Pakistan. How useful the Muslim support would have been if only they were here with us in an undivided India? Dalits with Muslims, Christians, Sikhs and Backward Castes, and the Mongoloid Tribes could have given the enemy a tough fight. But not only the "partition" got our stiffled voice muffled but the little remaining Muslims were further enfeebled because of their endless persecution. The Indian Muslims also started regretting the "partition". Since the Aryans (Hindus) consider Muslims as a separate nation and continue to kill them in hundreds in one after other bloodbath, we don't know for how long India's Muslims would tolerate this. We will not be surprised if there comes up another demand for a separate homeland for Muslims. India being a country of different nationalities, we will not be surprised with such a demand. When the people are demanding a separate Jharkhand, Uttarkhand, and Khalistan, the worst persecuted Muslims have every right to seek their own solution.

Be that as it may, the Indian "historians" have not yet unravelled the mysteries behind the "partition". Since these "historians" also happened to be upper castes we cannot expect them to speak out the truth. But whenever our historians come up with such works, would they keep quiet but expose the brahminical treachery behind this "partition" drama? The hideous role of Jawaharlal Nehru, Rajagopala-chari and even Gandhi? Therefore, we always have to depend upon foreign scholars for truth about India. Ayesha Jalal, a distinguished Cambridge scholar, has let the cat out of the bag when she says "It is the Congress Party that insisted on the partition. It was Jinnah who was against partition". (*Dalit Voice* Nov.1, 1985: *Truth on Partition of India*), Ayesha in her book, *The Sole Spokesman* (Cambridge University and Orient Longman, 1985) blasts the popular Hindu myth that it was the Muslims led by Jinnah who wanted Pakistan and it was Hindus who were forced to agree to the "partition."

Jinnah's greatness: One thing is clear from this book: Muslims were not originally keen about Pakistan. Jinnah was not the originator of the idea. He was a late convert in 1940, barely seven years before the birth of Pakistan. It was the "Socialist Brhamins" led by Nehru who found a heaven for them in such an idea. And we congratulate Godse for coming out with this truth. M.A. Jinnah, the tallest and the greatest Muslim leader of India, was a man of spotless character. He was originally in the Congress Party and never an orthodox Muslim. As a Sindhi, he did not know Urdu nor had he a beard. He had no trace of a "communal Muslim". The distinguished Barrister from Bombay was always in the company of non-Muslims. And how did this "Best ambassador of Hindu-Muslim unity" become the creator of Pakistan? (*Dalit Voice* Feb. 16, 1997 p.8: "*Hindu nazis made Jinnah communal and turn to Islam*"). The *Time* Magazine, (Dec. 23, 1996) made a cover story of Jinnah and paid tributes to the greatness of Jinnah. He was driven to despair and the nazi behaviour of the Indian upper castes convinced him that the "independence" would be a brahminical imperialism under which the Muslims would be choked to death. And hence it would be better if the Muslims sought separation - a point which Dr. Babasaheb Ambedkar also pleaded in his book, *Pakistan or Partition of India.*

We thank Godse for uncorking all these truths

> "Those who talk of India's freedom having been secured by Gandhi are not only ungrateful but are trying to write false history". (Godse book, p. 75).

The British wanted to quit India anyway and the changeover from the Conservative to the Labour Government hastened their exit. Besides, the Christian ethos itself was one that took into consideration the urges of the people. The British being Christians, that too Protestant Christians, they sympathised with the Indian demand for independence. But what did the Dalits of India achieve by this "independence"? Instead of the "foreign" exploiters we now have the "Aryan" exploiters.The Aryans came to India as the first invaders and if the rule that those who come first must quit first is applied, these Aryans will be affected first. Therefore, let not these Aryans call the British as foreigners.

Why no second Dr. Ambedkar: At least the "foreign" exploiters were much better. And Dr. Ambedkar could reach such heights and attain that stature only because of the British. This is exactly the reason why India has not produced a second Babasaheb Ambedkar. How could anybody breathe, let alone live, under this "Brahmin Raj"? So, even if Gandhi is given the credit for securing this "independence", we Dalits are not much thrilled by his achievement. No doubt, self-rule is better than a foreign rule but what have we gained by this "self-rule"? If this so-called self-rule comes in the way of our self-respect, we will not care for such a rule. The real self-rule will be achieved only when Dalits take over from the Aryan invaders and establish a Dalit Raj where everybody including the Brahmins can live in peace and dignity.

Multi-millionaire Gandhi: The fifth part of the Godse book begins with the bold sentence : "The day I decided to remove Gandhi from the political scene... " He knew that his action would make him the most hated man in India. But he was quite honest about it. To him what was important was not his reputation but the future of brahminism. He was critical of Gandhi "living in the palatial Birla House". Multi-millionaires of India had contributed huge funds to Gandhi. The Kasturba Fund and other Funds started by him attracted millions of rupees. Are the rich people bloody fools to pour money into Gandhi's basket? If they are fools why did they not give it to Dr. Ambedkar or to us? Wherever Gandhi went he was received and made to sit with millionaires.

Luxury of third class travel: To keep Gandhi in poverty, the Congress Party had to spend millions of rupees, said his own disciple, Mrs. Sarojini Naidu. When he travelled in third class, the entire compartment was reserved for him. If such is the luxury, we too don't mind travelling only in such a third class. Dr. Ambedkar had also made a similar comment on Gandhi's luxury and many "Socialist Brahmins" had then become furious about such a statement of a fact. They made another South Indian Brahmin, K.

Santhanam, (*The Hindustan Times*, New Delhi, 1946-pages 114) to write a vitriolic attack on Dr. Ambedkar's historical document, *What Congress and Gandhi Have Done to Untouchables*. For writing this book, Santhanam was made the Finance Minister in the first cabinet under Nehru. But when Dr. Ambedkar spoke the truth, the "Socialist Brahmins" became furious but now it is Godse who is saying the very same thing that Gandhi was financed by millionaires. When a Brahmin speaks even if it is untruth none utters a word against it. The Brahmin rule is that a Brahmin alone is capable of speaking the truth and nothing but the truth. He alone has the monopoly on truth. The others have no right to speak the truth.

Honesty of "Sacred Brahmins": Godse was fully convinced that Gandhi was the "greatest supporter and advocate of Pakistan". The remedy he decided was to kill Gandhi. And he did it. Should we not appreciate this Sacred Brahmin's sincerity? We may disagree with Godse but we can never doubt his sincerity. He was prepared to die for this. He said it and did exactly what he said. Not like our "Socialist Brahmins" who say Dalits and Muslims are our friends and then let loose the hounds on them. And when the hounds attack, they shed crocodile tears. Godse may be a Brahmin but he was an honest Brahmin. We like him. This breed of Brahmins is becoming a rarity. And more and more Brahmins are turning "Socialists" and dishonest. May the Godse tribe of Brahmins increase.

That is why even to this day RSS and many other "Sacred Brahmins" worship Godse. When Gandhi was killed they might have publicly mourned his death but they privately sympathised with Godse. During the *Gandhi* film show so much discussion was held in the press and the public but did anybody raise the question as to who killed Gandhi and why? To justify Godse killing Gandhi, they quoted their God Krishna's arguments to Arjuna that killing without malice and without any selfish gain is sacred. Godse killed Gandhi as a sacred duty to fulfil a mission. "I have resorted to the action I did purely for the benefit of the **humanity**", (p. 112 of Godse book) he says defending his killing of Gandhi. Look at the courage of his conviction.

To a Brahmin "**humanity**" is restricted to his community. That means to save brahminism, Godse killed Gandhi.

> "There was no legal machinery by which such an offender could be brought to book and it was therefore that I resorted to firing of shots at Gandhi as that was the only meet thing to do". (p. 113).

Is there any Brahmin who can disagree with this? If so, has anybody come out with any statement to that effect? Rather they rejoiced over the killing of Gandhi by distributing sweets. Even today within the RSS *shakas*, they distribute sweets on the day Gandhi was killed. Godse wanted no mercy. He admitted having killed Gandhi and also boldly narrated the reasoning behind it.

***Gita* defends murder:** By this statement Godse is putting forward a Hindu philosophical interpretation to his killing of Gandhi. This killing of Gandhi is not a simple affair between two individuals. It has a deep philosophical and historical implication which God Krishna expounds in the *Gita*, which the Hindus hold as holy as the Vedas, the highest of their sacred scriptures. Krishna tells Arjuna in the *Gita*, which was Gandhi's bedside Bible, to kill Kauravas. He asks Arjuna to fight and kill. Arjuna is hesitating to kill his close relatives. To this the god replies in the famous oft-repeated Sanskrit passage: "*Karmanye vadikarasthe ma phaleshu kadachana*" (*Gita* verse 3-8). The god orders Arjuna to fight and kill, unmindful of the consequences, to root out the evil and establish the *dharma*. Hence god himself is here advocating that "action without any desire for the fruit is superior to abstention from action". Killing is also told as part of the caste duties of a Kashatriya. B.G. Tilak in his famous book on the *Gita* also says that killing is sanctioned under Hinduism to protect *dharma*. Violence is fully sanctioned under Hinduism. Krishna also tells Arjuna to kill without malice, ill - will, love or hate. Killing should have no selfish motive. Arjuna had nothing personal against the Kauravas, Godse had nothing personal against Gandhi. Beant Singh also had nothing personal against Indira Gandhi (DV Edit Dec. 16, 1984: *"Why Beant Singh killed Mrs. Indira Gandhi?"*). Each did it to establish *dharma*, according to them.

Godse had expressed his desire that the divided India would again get united. That would indeed be a wonderful dream. But since then even Pakistan got divided and Bangladesh became separate. And Godse's own party has given up the *Akhand Bharat* slogan.

RSS goodbye to *Bunch of Thoughts*: Our point is this country has seen worse leaders than Gandhi but why RSS did not kill them? Is it because they were Brahmins? Why the RSS has changed its "honest" policy? Why did they discard their own nazi philosopher's book, *Bunch of Thoughts* (1996, Jagarana Prakashana, Kempe Gowda Nagar, Bangalore - 560 019). The book is not only relegated to background but not even sold by the RSS. Why this dishonesty? Why the Gandhi-killers later turned into Gandhi admirers? Nay, the custodians of Gandhi and gandhism? Is it based on the Brahmin philosophy that every revolutionary should be condemned while alive, everything should be done to liquidate him but worshipped only after that revolutionary is dead? They did this with the Budha, Gandhi and now they are trying it with Dr. Ambedkar as well.

If the RSS policy is guided by the RSS Bible, *Bunch of Thoughts*, how the RSS shifted to "gandhian socialism" as its political philosophy? Is the RSS also going away from its honest "Sacred Brahmin" policy and following Gandhi's policy of double-dealing, double-talk and double-cross? Is the RSS also trying to become dishonest because that alone will fetch them votes? Is it a trick to deceive the masses? Whatever it is, the RSS is undergoing a big change. So too the "Socialist Brahmins". Who will swallow whom is to be watched. But the events since then have proved that it is the "Socialist Brahmins" who derive all the advantages by attacking the "Sacred Brahmins" . Since both represent the same stock of Aryan upper castes - it is now becoming clear that the "Sacred Brahmins" act as the shock absorbers of the "Socialist Brahmins."

VI - NATIONALISM & HINDUISM

Every religion in the world has a founder, a sacred text, a set of beliefs, practices and a fixed theology. Any deviation from these results in the loss of that religion. Ahmadias or Quadianis, a sect among Muslims, have been declared "non-Muslims" by a concord of Islamic scholars of the whole world because they are said to have deviated from the belief that Prophet Mohamad is the last of the prophets, even though Ahamadias believe in all other matters of Islam and strictly follow all Islamic injunctions.

Dalits forcibly called Hindus: But what is known as "Hinduism" has no definition, no single sacred text, no set of beliefs and no set of practices. Whether a man believes in one good or a million gods, or an athiest; whether he is a beef-eater, vegetarian, a worshipper of Vishnu, Shiva or a seprent, he is considered a Hindu not by himself but by the Brahmins, the Indian Government and the law of the land. The Sikhs, Lingayats, Budhists and Jains do not consider themselves Hindus and yet the Constitution of India, the various Hindu Acts passed by the Indian Parliament like the Hindu Marriages Act etc. and the upper caste bureaucracy declare that they are Hindus. When the Dalits started asserting under the leadership of Dr Ambedkar that they were a distinct people different from the Hindus, like the Muslims and Christians, they were compelled under threats of a fast-unto-death by Gandhi that they could not call themselves non-Hindus. The central point of the Gandhi-Ambedkar pact (Poona Pact) of 1932 was that the Scheduled Castes (the name used in the Constitution for Untouchables) must remain within the fold of Hinduism. (V.T. Rajshekar: *Separate Electorate & Separate Settlement*, Dalit Sahitya Akademy, 1996).

What exactly is Hinduism? The so-called sacred scriptures of Hindus do not mention any of the words - Hindu, Hinduism or Hindustan. These words are derived from the word *Hindu*, which is a Persian word meaning Indian, thief, dacoit, slave. It is also said that the word *Hindu* is derived from the word *Sindhu* (Indus). Whatever it is the word is not a Hindu or an Indian word. This word assumed importance during the Muslim rule of India of about 1,000 years when all the Indians except the Muslims, Christians and Parsis, Sikhs, Budhists and Jains were considered by the Muslim rulers as Hindus for purposes of identification.

Nazi cult: The same identification was followed by the British. But during the "freedom movement", the word assumed political significance, and taking hints from the idea of "nationalism" preached by European political scientists, a "Hindu nationalism" was artificially created, which later developed into a nazi cult.

All attempts are being made in India now to project "Hinduism" as a philosophy, a religion, a proud institution, the world's oldest civilization, a deliverer of human needs, a glorious cultural heritage and what not. The "Hindus", who had been on the retreat for the past over 1,000 years, hanging their heads in shame, are trying to fool the world about their greatness. India's ruling class is squandering billions of rupees through "Indian Fairs" in Europe and America, through nudity, free sex, music, drugs, opium and hashish, Hare Krishna street dances to propagate and popularise Hinduism. Outside India and within India through films, TV, radio, monopoly press, textbooks, seminars and above all through anti-Muslim, anti-Sikh and anti-Christian riots and all other propaganda means it is bending backwards to spread Hinduism. And this Hinduism is nothing but a nazi doctrine, "Give a common enemy to the masses and they will fight it on your behalf". This policy of hating the "religious minorities" is not just to contain and confound the "minorities", but to tell all "others" (non-minorities) that they are "Hindus" and as "Hindus" they are different from others, and that they as the "majority community" become the rulers of India. When it says that the Muslim population is multiplying in India, it should be taken as a warning to "Hindus" : beware, by this pace of increase, Hindus will become a minority in India in a few decades. And a "Hindu" believes what he wants to believe.

Hindu belief system: If one wants to see the working of such a Hindu belief system, one must come to India. In this country anything stupid, irrational, unreasonable or unscientific is believed and they are even prepared to spend any amount of money and even die owing to this belief system. In no other country "holymen" are such thugs and pindaris. These scoundrels in the guise of holy men deceive the gullible Hindus and become billionaires because they know that the Hindu belief system will not allow them to develop a questioning, rational, scientific mind. A Hindu accepts anything and everything even if it is illogical, unreasonable and blatantly false. Hundreds of frauds are today parading all over India as saints.

Gandhi, "a devout Hindu", knew this and made the best use of the Hindu mind and exploited this blind belief and sentiments. And the superstitious Hindus raised him to *mahatmahood* that gave him licence to loot the masses and promote upper caste interests which every godman has been doing from the beginning.

Majority afraid of minority: This "Hindu" is kept under a constant fear of his very existence. India is the only country in the world where the "majority" population is mortally afraid of the "minorities". So many Hindu nazi organisations like the RSS, Vishwa Hindu Parishad, Virat Hindu Samaj, Hindu Mahasabha, Bajrang Dal, Hindu Munnani, Shiv Sena etc have been formed to defend the "majority" (Hindus). Do the Muslims of Pakistan or Bangladesh or the Budhists of Burma have any para-military organisations in their countries to defend their religion against their minorities?

According to these Hindus, they form 85% of the population. And the non-Hindus are just 15% and yet this brute majority is afraid of its minorities. Nowhere in the world a "majority" community is afraid of its "minorities" except in India. Why? The Muslims, Sikhs, Christians, Nagas and other "minorities" like Dalits and Tribals may not know the answer, but the "Hindu" knows it. The "Hindu" knows that his "Hinduism" is declining, decaying and disappearing. No day the sun rises in India without some

"Hindus" bidding good-bye to Hinduism by embracing Islam, Christianity, Budhism or Sikhism. The "Hindu" knows that when Prophet Mohammed preached Islam in Arabia, the whole of this sub-continent of India was "Hindu" and gradually and systematically the Hindus started deserting Hinduism; and on the day the "Hindu rule" was re-established in India in 1947, about 15% of Indians (Hindus) were out of the Hindu fold and they were Muslims. The "Hindu" fear is that if he waits for a few more decades, he will be outdone. And if the Muslims decide, they might annul Pakistan and Bangladesh, merge them into India, and then if it becomes a reality the Muslims will become a majority. And even democratically through the strength of numbers, the "Hindus" will be outbeaten and reduced to a minority.

***Vaidik* bid to divide India:** That is why the once fond Hindu nazi slogan of *Akhand Bharat* (United India of pre-1947) is no longer heard. It has mysteriously disappeared. Nobody utters this slogan even by mistake. In fact the *vaidik* vampire is bent upon further dividing India by driving out the Sikhs, Kashmirs and the North-East mongoloid tribals. But the non-Hindu majority - SC/ ST/ BCs and Muslim/Christian/Sikhs - who form over 85% of India's population - are firmly against further vivisection of India. *Akhand Bharat* will amount to rule of Muslims and subjugation of Hindus. That is why so many Hindu nazi organisations have sprung up to "defend" Hinduism. What a pity that bodyguards are kept to defend the Tarzan in his own house.

Gandhi in his book, *An Autobiography*, (Navajivan Publications , Ahmedabad-380014) admitted that he failed to cross-examine a witness in his first and last case in Bombay and was ultimately selected by a Muslim, Dada Abdulla of South Africa, and introduced to his attorneys. Except the Muslims, other Indians were not allowed to wear turbans in the South African courts. So, when the unself-respecting Gandhi decided to give up his turban and wear the English hat, Dada Abdulla gave Gandhi the first lesson in patriotism and advised him not to give up self-respect. After this lesson, one after other South African Indian

Muslims like Adamji Miyakhan, Haji Khan Mohammed, Seth Abdul Ghani, Mohammad Kasam Kamruddin taught him politics and the art of leadership and gave at their expenses publicity and encouragement. And that is how Gandhi became a leader and earned a lot of reputation (pages 89 to 98. 14th reprint). That means Gandhi was originally helped by the Muslims though he turned ungrateful later.

Born out of *papayoni*: When he came back to India, his Bania (trader) caste became the greatest hindrance. Brahmin leaders like Tilak, Gokhale and Motilal Nehru, who were then controlling the Hindu politics, were not prepared to join hands with a man lower down in caste hierarchy. How could a non-Brahmin that too born out of *papayoni* lead the Brahmins? This is something the Brahmins deeply resented. It was during this crisis he was picked up and brought forward by a great leader of the time, Moulana Mohammed Ali, in his Khilafat Movement. Gandhi was taken round the whole of India under the leadership of Mohammed Ali with Khilafat funds and made to address Muslim gatherings. He was nicknamed "mahatma" for his "contribution" to the Muslim cause by the Ali Brothers. Gandhi thus was initially made by Muslims. And once he became an all-India figure, achieved name and fame, he kicked the ladder and the "Hindu" leadership thought of exploiting this crafty Bania for their cause and snatched him from the hands of Muslims. And Gandhi true to his Bania salt, betrayed the Muslims, joined the Brahmins and in his loyalty to Brahmins became more loyal than the king himself and saved "Hinduism" from total extinction from the world scene.

✿ ✿ ✿ ✿

VII - HINDU-MUSLIM MARRIAGES: TREND REVERSED

Ever since the Muslim rule was consolidated in India, the practice of the Muslim rulers and the Muslim elites was to amalgamate with the Hindus through matrimonial ties. The Islamic law permitted the marriage of Muslim men with the women of *Ahle-Kitab*. The law-givers in West Asia had declared only Christians and Jews as *Ahle-Kitab*, but later the Muslims considered the Hindus also as *Ahle-Kitab* instead of as *Kafars* or idol-worshippers and legitimised the marriage with Hindu women. Many great historical personalities were children of such marriages, their mothers being Hindus. The names of Mohamad-bin-Tughluk, Amir Khusro, Mughal Emperors Jahangir and Shahjahan are given here to show how the children of Hindu mothers have to be honourably accepted by the Muslims.

According to Muslim sources it was Gandhi who tried to put an end to this practice. Rather, he tried to reverse the trend, i.e. to encourage marriages of Muslim women with Hindu men. He successfully prevented Vijayalakshmi, Jawaharlal Nehru's sister (later Vijayalakshmi Pundit), from living with her lover, Syed Hussain. Vijayalakshmi, a Kashmiri Brahmin, had embraced Islam at the hands of Moulana Fajiz of Allahabad and performed the *nikah* with Syed Hussain. Gandhi protested against this and even threatened that the alliance would break the Hindu-Muslim unity. Gandhi did not rest till this marriage was broken and after giving intensive "spiritual training" to her in his *ashram* got her married to S.K. Pundit, and Syed Hussain migrated to USA (*Hayat-e-Md. Ali Jinnah* -R.A. Jaferi, p. 702-703, Taj Office Book Depot, Bombay-1946).

His coming in the way of two lovers could have been overlooked in the interest of political exigencies. But when a Muslim girl, Rahana Tayab, daughter of Abbas Tayabji, married a Hindu of the Shankar Lal Banker family in Berlin in 1929, Gandhi betrayed his eagerness by sending a cable to her wishing her all prosperity and happiness (Ibid-p. 703). Thus Gandhi tried to reverse the trend of Hind-Muslim marriages.

The followers of Gandhi continued this trend set by their mentor. The cry for a common civil code in India heard all over India is an indirect way through which they dream to create a mentality of ignoring the religious sanctity in matrimonial purpose so that the Muslim women may be taken as their wives, as the marriage of Rehana Tayab with a Hindu received the blessings of the *mahatma*.

Conversion to Islam: Islam has been a missionary religion and the Muslims feel thrilled when a non-Muslim gets converted to Islam. This has been a continuous process. But Gandhi expressed great displeasure over this trend and tried to reverse it. When Dr. Iqbal's friend, Kanhiyalal Gauba, a barrister, embraced Islam and became Khalid Latif Gauba, Gandhi paid a special visit to Lahore and tried his best to reconvert him to Hinduism (*shuddhi*). And when his own son, Hiralal Gandhi, embraced Islam the *mahatma* hurled the choicest abuses and launched all sorts of vile propaganda against his son putting the world to a surprise as to why all these defects of his son were exposed only then.

The role played by Gandhi during and after the Round Table Conference of 1931 to keep the Dalits (Untouchables) within the Hindu religion is the most heinous crime that he committed against our people. The Dalits were neither allowed to have a separate identity for themselves like the Muslims, Christians and Sikhs nor were they allowed to join other religions. They were compelled to accept their lowest status and remain as Hindus and rot within. Dr. B.R. Ambedkar in many of his writings has said how the Dalit mental weakness, illiteracy, poverty, scattered population throughout the length and breadth of India, lack of leadership and disunity were fully exploited by Gandhi. Dr. Ambedkar was compelled not by the use of rhetoric and intellect but by the treacherous and cowardly weapon of fast-unto-death threats that if Gandhi really died as a result of this fast, there would be mass murders of the Dalits all over India. Dr. Ambedkar had to finally surrender not before wisdom, justice and bravery but before cowardice, obstinacy, blackmail and arrogance.

Never before in history a straight-forward, brave, intellectually honest person was defeated by a coward employing arrogance, deception and blackmail as Dr. Ambedkar by Gandhi. Gandhi's wife, Kasturba, came to Dr. Ambedkar begging him to "save" her *mangal sutra* (a chain round a women's neck used as a sign that her husband is alive). Dr. Ambedkar had to give up his principle, forced to betray his own deprived, poverty - stricken community of Untouchables - forming a third of India's population - to save the life of the "Father of Nation" so that the upper castes who rule India are not deprived of their slaves.

But Dr. Ambedkar by his sagacity and intellectual superiority still defeated Gandhi by wrenching from him certain "reservations", which he got not as a dole, generosity, charity or concession but as an honourable settlement - a pact - the "Poona Pact". Only an agreement between two "nations" is called a pact and the "Poona Pact" was also between two "nations" of Hindus and Untouchables. And the two continues to be different nations, if not opposite poles, even after 65 years of signing this "Poona Pact".

Gujarat "caste wars": Billions of rupees have been spent and thousands of pages have been printed to confuse and convince the world outside and the Dalits inside that it is Gandhi who is the "saviour" of Dalits and it is because of him untouchability is abolished. The propaganda is also so loud that it was Gandhi who secured the "reservations" and all those concessions so that the Hindus could wash off their sins of torturing the Dalits and that it was an act of repentance. This is yet another gandhian trick to snatch away the credit from Dr. Ambedkar. It is also an attempt to withdraw the constitutional reservations of the Dalits whenever the Hindus feel that their "washing ceremony" is over. The two major "caste wars" (1981 & 1985) the followers of Gandhi waged in his home state of Gujarat should serve as a warning to us that those who have "given the reservations" have also the right to take it back. The concessions also enabled the Hindus to keep the Dalits within the Hindu fold.

"Epic fast" to ruin Dalits: What Dr. Ambedkar, however, demanded from the British and the British were prepared to give, was not "reservations" but a "separate electorate". The Brahmins feared that a separate electorate for Dalits would help make Dr. Ambedkar the first prime minister of India, and it is this fear that made them to persuade Gandhi to go on a fast-unto-death against the Dalits. That means out of the 32 "fasts unto death" he had undertaken in his life time not a single fast was devoted to support the Dalits. But he did undertake at least one fast, that is the "Epic Fast", to ruin our people.

The Muslims also put forward certain demands before the British and they got it because they were more organised than the Dalits. Gandhi tried to hoodwink the Muslims and also through various offers. But the Muslims refused to trust him. But the Dalits could not fight Gandhi at that time. Though they had a towering leader in Babasaheb Ambedkar, his followers were not capable of performing their duties. Besides, the extraordinarily efficient brahminical corrupting and co-opting machinery worked overtime to woo a large number of *Harijans* away from Dr. Ambedkar. M.C. Raja, a Tamil *Harijan*, was purchased by Gandhi's Hindu followers to fight Babasaheb. A fellow who was an ardent supporter of separate electorate became a Gandhi stooge over might. (*Dr. Babasaheb Ambedkar Writings & Speeches* Vol. 5 p.356, Govt. of Maharashtra, 1989).

Dr. Ambedkar called anti-national: The Untouchable masses did not have the mental capacity to understand and appreciate the words of wisdom of Dr Ambedkar. Babasaheb himself expressed these feelings at the fag end of his life. His enemies understood him so well and did everything to scuttle him. But his own children did not know him and those who knew him could not understand him. Gandhi was used by the Indian ruling class to do this job. So much so, a large mass of Dalits came under the spell of Gandhi. The mass media and the history book-writers at that time played the heinous role of suppressing the truth-painting Gandhi as the saviour of *Harijans* and taunting Dr. Ambedkar as anti-national.

Blessed by Gandhi, the Hindus today are preparing the ground to withdraw the "reservations" any time. They have forgotten that the "Poona Pact" of 1932 is a pact between two nations - the nation of Hindus and the nation of Dalits.

The "Poona Pact" provided Gandhi yet another stick to beat the Dalits. It blocked the conversion of Dalits to Islam, Christianity and even Budhism. That is why the moment a Dalit gives up Hinduism, he or she is deprived of the "reservations" which are used as a bribe to keep our people as Hindus. The very Constitution of India is being used to promote Hinduism. So, the "reservations" is a major contribution of Gandhi to save Hinduism and the Hindus becoming a minority in India.

Hinduisation of Dalits: India's "national" toilet papers are trying to convince their readers that it is the RSS-BJP Hindu nazi parties that are advocates of *hindutva* and that Gandhi and gandhism stood for secularism and national unity. This is a big lie. *Vaidik Dharma*, renamed as Hinduism, would have died just at the time India got "independence" and the credit for saving this religion of the rulers goes to Gandhi and not to the Hindu nazi parties.

India's different *vaidik* nazi leaders belonged to the honest "Sacred Brahmin" category and had they been allowed to have their way, they would have sharpened the caste and religious contradictions and paved the way for the surfacing of different submerged nationalities and also thereby trampling Hinduism in the process. Gandhi and his "Socialist Brahmin" advisers scented this danger. Dr Ambedkar's separate electorate would have taken the Untouchables and Tribals not only out of Hinduism but made them the deadliest foes of Hinduism. Through the "Poona Pact", the wily Bania averted this danger and saved his Hindus and Hinduism. And such a *hinduisation* (enslavement) of Untouchables and Tribals is today taken up on a war-footing by the gandhians, and Hindu nazis and the government itself controlled by Hindus. Such a *hinduisation* of non-Hindu Dalits (20%), Tribals (10%) is serving as a double-edged weapon for the Hindus. On one side it is keeping 30% of the population forcibly under Hinduism, enabling the Hindus to tell the world that Hindus constitute 85% of the population. And on the other this sword is helping the Hindus to fight the Muslims, Sikhs and Christians.

Bengali Dalit achievement: Gandhi feared that once the Dalits became Muslims, Christians, Sikhs or Budhists they would get liberated from Hinduism and that in turn would inspire them to seek political liberation. Bengali Dalits, converted to Islam, today have a separate Muslim nation of their own - Bangladesh. But their counterparts in West Bengal, their own blood relations forced to remain within the Hindu fold, continue as Untouchables even to this day. Since the problem of Untouchables is not economic but social and cultural, religious conversion has become a major tool for liberation. (Dr. B.R. Ambedkar: *Why Go For Conversion?* Dalit Sahitya Akademy, 1987). Dr. Ambedkar himself resorted to this by embracing Budhism. But Gandhi effectively blocked the liberation of Dalits. So much so our people, as slaves, are cooped up as sub-humans within the dungeon of Hinduism - neither living nor dead. In other words, the credit for saving Hinduism and converting India into a *Hindu Rashtra* goes to this Gujarati Bania and not to any Hindu nazi party.

Liberation thru Islam: The nervousness displayed by the upper castes upon the mass conversion of a few hundred Dalits to Islam in Meenakshipuram (Tamil Nadu) is a pointer to this. The Hindu fear is that the separate Tamil National movement which they successfully curbed through communal, caste and language intrigues, cannot be curbed if Islam intervenes and liberates the Dalits.

Gandhi perhaps had forseen all these developments and tried his best to put an end to these once and for all. But Gandhi did not know that the big hole at the bottom of the Hindu ship could not be plugged by such a patchwork. The ship should be allowed to sink and a new ship built.

Will the Hindu nazis abondon their sinking ship and take refuge in a new ship or will they prefer to be drowned with the sinking ship? When history takes stock of Gandhi, it will get any number of evidences to prove that "Socialist Brahmins" voted for the second alternative but it was Godse, the "Sacred Brahmin", who opted for the first.

Greatness of Godse: Godse was an honest *vaidik*. And we like all such people. We have no quarrel with them because they don't interfere with our lives nor do we interfere with their secluded lives. India is ruled by *gandhiwadis* - his followers. Barring the BJP, the Hindu nazi party, almost all "national" political parties are Gandhi followers. Every prime minister has been a gandhian. So, these gandhians have to be given the credit if India is what it is today - a beggar country, laughing stock of the whole world. All-round corruption, environmental degradation, urban boom and rural decay, total breakdown of law and order have converted India into a functioning anarchy. Gandhi and gandhians did this. Godse and his "Sacred Brahmins" cannot be blamed for it. The ruling upper castes (15%) are hugging hard to Gandhi and gandhism because they became rulers because of Gandhi and gandhism. They might be ungrateful to Gandhi, they might have forgotten the Father of their upper caste nation but they will never give up gandhism because that brought them enormous benefits all-round.

That is why all those who are interested in saving India including the honest "Sacred Brahmins", if there are any, must first finish Gandhi and gandhism - rather than directing their energies to fight Hindu nazis. These Hindu nazis are our open, honest enemies and when caste identity strengthens and caste contradictions automatically get sharpened, Hindu nazis will automatically die. We need not kill the Hindu nazis. These nazis will kill each other. The enemies of Hinduism are within Hinduism itself. We need not bother about them.

VIII - GANDHI, A FRIEND OF MUSLIMS ?

Before joining the brahminical camp in his pre-1921 days, Gandhi was said to be a liberal but after this he turned a Hindu leader through adopting a dual policy, double-tongue, say something and do exactly the opposite. Even as pretending to be a friend of Muslims, he outdid Kautilya's tactics and subtly created the Hindu-Muslim rift. By always harping on the "Hindu-Muslim unity", he indirectly drove home the point that Indians are divided into Hindus and Muslims. All shades of Hindu nazis secretly took his advice in the art of his dual politics. His first pro-Hindu nazi act was to reject the "complete independence" resolution moved by Moulana Hasrat Mohani in the 1921 Ahmedabad session of the Congress Party. The same resolution was later passed in the 1927 Madras session and this became the creed of the Congress in the 1929 Lahore session (P.C. Mitra - "Salute to a Patriot", *Deccan Herald*, 10.5.1981). What happened between 1921 and 1927 is worth noting to assess Gandhi's anti-Muslim role.

Till 1921, the Indian political scene was dominated by the Muslims. Great stalwarts like the Ali Brothers, Hasrath Mohani, Jinnah and Moulana Azad were holding the reins of Indian politics. The Hindu political giants who succeeded were dwarfs before these giants. The independence of India in those days meant the genuine rule of Indians, not of the Hindus or Muslims. And of course, the Muslims with their superior intellectual and political qualities would have dominated the scene and built up an India, where the Brahmins would have been insignificant as during their earlier rule. So, Gandhi wanted a breathing time during which the Hindus would organise themselves to become a force to reckon with and he succeeded in achieving his object within 10 years. By 1931, the Hindus (meaning the Aryans or upper castes) were organised enough to outdo the Muslims not in political acumen, but by convincing the gullible masses that the "Hindus" are a majority and Muslims are a "minority" and as a minority the Muslims must learn to be ruled by the majority.

Muslims not a minority: The pity is that the leadership of the oppressed Muslim community, having been corrupted and coopted by the ruling upper castes, has convinced the community that Muslims are a "minority". Here is a case of a community leadership itself injecting inferiority complex into its community. We had reminded the Muslim leadership repeatedly that Muslims are not a "minority" as propagated by the Hindus but the country's single largest community - if not the single most explosive community. But this explosive stuff is kept in the cold storage and allowed to freeze by the community's corrupt leadership. But thanks to the oppressed Muslim masses, this leadership stands rejected. In Kerala, West Bengal and Assam, Muslims form a sizeable population, much more than the all-India average of 15%, but the upper castes have kept them as slaves. Muslims in these three states have the power, the strength to choke the throat of their oppressors but the Muslim leadership is restraining them. The upper caste twist of facts and the Muslim leadership repeating this nonsense that Muslims are a "minority" is restraining the masses from hitting back.

Muslims are not a "minority" but India's single largest community. Nay. Muslims are India's one and the only **community**. The rest are castes, tribes and ethnic identities. As the country's only **community**, and in fact the country's single largest community, the Muslims are in a position to dictate things. But their corrupted and co-opted leadership made this community a slave of the upper castes. (*Curse of Allah*, Dalit Sahitya Akademy, 1997).

Siege mentality grips Hindus: Why the Hindus are spreading this falsehood that Muslims are a "minority" and Hindus, who are not even 15% of the population, are a big "majority"? Obviously, this is because of a siege mentality that has gripped the Aryan upper castes. The *vaidik* vampire is in a state of desperate uncertainty. The Aryans have no "nation" of their own to migrate and inside India they are under constant threat. Hence this utter sense of inferiority that has gripped the "Hindu mind" having been under centuries of Muslim rule. The Indo-

Islamic culture was the culture of the whole of North India from Khyber Pass to the borders of Bengal. This culture was closer to the culture of Iran and Afghanistan than it was to the rest of India.

Arya Samaj movement: Gandhi advised Swamy Shradhananda to spread the Arya Samaj movement, which took birth in Gujarat, to Punjab and UP where the "Hindu" was a better product of Islamic culture than a Muslim in the rest of India. Through the Arya Samaj, a Hindu revivalist cultural revolution was to be brought about in the North Indian (*Arya Varta*) region which today is called the Hindu (cow) belt. The modus operandi was to spread a canard against Muslims and Muslim mannerisms in all fields including eating, speaking, bathing, dressing, singing, marriage laws and every aspect of individual and social life of the Muslims. And "Hindus" were advised to give up everything that had an Islamic touch. The *shuddhi* (purification) movement started in 1922 by Shradhananda had Gandhi's blessings. This movement was started to "reconvert" the Muslims to Hinduism by performing their *shuddhi* as they were originally Hindus but forcibly polluted by Islam. Similarly Madan Mohan Malaviya, a UP Brahmin, received full support from Gandhi to organise an anti-Muslim para-military force, *Sanghatan*. All these organisations took birth and grew under the patronage of the *mahatma* as they are intended to develop political consciousness among the Indians, meaning the non-Muslim masses.

How the Muslims reacted to these movements and what was the ultimate result of these movements and counter-movements is not our concern. Our concern is only to show that because of Gandhi's support to these Hindu revivalist movements, "Hinduism" as a political force was activised. Gandhi helped Hindus to shed their inferiority complex and become militant, which after "independence" assumed the form of a cult resembling Hitler's nazi style. Therefore, history may rightly conclude that it was Gandhi who saved Hinduism and not any Hindu nazi party like the RSS.

Rise of anti-Brahmin movements: The net result of a 1,000-year Muslim rule had completely paralysed the "Hindu" mind. The initial fervour shown by the Adi Shankara on the religious level and Prithviraj on the political power had brought about a complete spiritual and cultural change in the country. Powerful anti-Brahmin (Hindu) movements like the Malik Kafoor's (a Dalit convert commander-in-chief of Allauddin Khilji), breaking of temple and Hindu gods and demons, growth of the Bhakti cult in which the Vedas and other religious scriptures were totally rejected, birth of such great anti-Brahmin protest religions like the Veerashaivism in the South and Sikhism in the North had inflicted wound after wound upon the fragile body of Hinduism.

Brahmins welcome British rule: Hinduism itself was about to die forever when the British came giving a breathing time badly needed for Hinduism. The British rule was a "god sent" blessing for the upper castes, and the Brahmins contributed the most in enlisting support of the East India Company in its bid to capture power from the Muslims. It is they who put into the British brain the idea that both were Aryans. The White-skinned British were flattered when they were called Aryans and they founded a Chair for Sanskrit at Oxford University. So, the Aryans of Europe and the Aryans of India lived in perfect understanding jointly exploiting and plundering the natives of the land despite warnings by many dedicated Christian missionaries. But this too proved temporary. The non-Aryan Bengali Hindus took this opportunity of Calcutta becoming the capital of India to save themselves from the Aryan yoke and started such "un-Hindu" activities like beef-eating clubs, prevention of *sati*, widow marriage and imitation and propagation of Western mannerisms and thoughts. Raja Rammohan Roy, a Bengali Brahmin, became a great friend of the British and, through his Hindu reform movement called Brahmo Samaj, tried to westernise the people. The Hindus said Christianity hated Islam but not Hinduism. Their only consolation was "we need not be afraid of Muslims any more as the Christians have come to our rescue."

Three enemies of Hinduism: The result : Hinduism was about to lose ground against Christianity. Gandhi's activities removed this inferiority from the Hindu mind and Hinduism was projected as a philosophy, a way of life, a means of deliverance and what not. He used all the three enemies of Hinduism - mysticism, militarism and political revivalism - to save Hinduism, to revive Hinduism and thus became the saviour of Hinduism.

But poor Gandhi was mistaken. What he gave in the form of mysticism, dressed as a half-naked fakir, was not spiritual mysticism but showy mysticism, which within a short time started showing its hollowness and treachery through such fake mystics like Rajneesh, Satya Sai Baba, Chinmayananda and other bhagwans, acharyas and swamis, who brought greater disgrace to Hinduism than anybody else in the past. His militarism degenerated to cruelty and violence of the worst type. More Indians have been killed in "independent" India in anti-Muslim, anti-Sikh, caste wars, police-firing on agitating, half-naked, starving masses, torture in police stations and killings in religious places than those killed during all the battles under the Muslim and British rules. His political revivalism vested all power in Brahmin bureaucrats and Bania capitalists, who remained miles away from the Indian masses than the Muslim emperors or the British viceroys who were more accessible to the masses. Political leaders became powerless as power is not vested in them but in bureaucrats who confine themselves to their air-conditioned chambers amassing wealth.

Thus, the pseudo-spiritualism of the pseudo-saints (product of gandhian pseudo-mysticism), militarism (products of *sanghatanism*), and Hindu nationalism (indoctrinated by gandhian political revivalism), have jointly created a force which may appear to superficial observers as the saviour of Hinduism, but in reality this combination of the three has brought about such a disaster never before faced by Hinduism. Through these three "isms", Hinduism has been given a *Trishul* (trident) with which it may get temporary victories against the Muslims but in the end it may commit suicide with the same *Trishul*. And that end is not far off.

Fall of Hindutva heroes: Hindus are great admirers of gandhism, and gandhism itself has become synonymous with Hinduism. And it is these nazi *hindutva* heroes who demolished the Babri masjid (1992) thinking that by stabbing the very heart of the Muslim, they would be able to "rouse" the Hindus, "unite" the Hindus and let loose the Hindu hounds agianst the Muslims. But did this happen? In all the subsequent elections, the Hindu nazi parties lost and even in the 1996 general elections when the BJP emerged as the single largest party, all the rest of the parties ganged up against it and pulled down its short-lived, 14-day old govt. headed by the *Vaidik* A.B. Vajpayee. The Hindu nazi parties have called off their anti-Muslim rhetorics at least temporarily. That means the *gandhiwadis* and Hindu wadis are gaining nothing by mouthing anti-Muslim slogans and spilling Muslim blood. Besides this, the caste contradictions inside the Hindu nazi parties have created big divisions within the largest Hindu nazi party. The worst enemies of the Hindu nazi party are within that party itself. That is how the Hindu nazi party lost its rule over Gujarat and its own followers did not allow the party to come to power in UP. That means gandhism, Hinduism and nazism (all the three meaning the same) have reached their climax and the decline has begun.

IX - GANDHI SAVED HINDUISM

What was the image of India in the civilised part of the world before Gandhi came on the scene? Those in the West used to consider India as a land of hunger, beggars, snake-charmers, epidemic diseases, naked monks, black magic, witchcraft, "sacred cows" wandering on busy streets and maharajas going on caparisoned elephants wading through starving mobs. This was the picture of India then though by and large the image continues. Rarely a historian or writer had taken India seriously. The British could control this whole sub-continent with three army garrisons, one each at Calcutta, Bombay and Madras. A land of absolute cowards. Its so-called religion, Hinduism, was a bundle of confusion to foreigners. Anybody could interpret it anyway one liked. It was like that seven blind men and the elephant. It was utter chaos. So much so, no body had any good opinion of India, much less its religion of Hinduism.

Vivekananda might have done something to present a rosy picture to the Western world but he was not a man of the masses. He was too big a philosopher for the common man to understand whether in India or outside. But it was Gandhi who for the first time brought respectability to Hinduism and made the civilised part of the world to rethink and re-evaluate Hinduism.

Biggest bluff of 20th century: Gandhi was more a Hindu monk with a political garb. His was a double-edged weapon which he used against the British. His fight against the British empire was political but he used religion to fight them without saying so. It was Gandhi who popularised Hindu and hinduism in the whole world. And it was he who said that Hinduism stood for non-violence and tolerance - the biggest bluff of the 20th century.

Before coming to India, he used to wear stitched-in-London full-suit, a Western dress. But after coming to India he changed his sartorial style in his true Chanakya fashion. By chanting Hindu gods' names and using simple words to explain religious ideas to masses, he captured the superstitious masses and impressed upon them that no socio-economic reform was possible without driving the British out.

His methods perfectly suited not only the exploiting upper castes but even some lower below. It perfectly fitted with the native cunningness of the Hindu. The *vaidik dharma*, being the other word for exploitation, makes everyone of its follower an expert exploiter. Like every big fish wanting to eat the smaller one, in India every poor Hindu wants to become rich by exploiting those lower down. That is why no "poor" man in India hates the rich because he in turn wants to become rich. That is why there is no "class struggle" in India by which Karl Marx means a clash between the exploited and the exploiter. To such a nation of exploiters, barring of course the Untouchables and Tribals who are at the lowest rung of the Indian society and hence none below to exploit, Gandhi gave a political interpretation of Hinduism perfectly tailor-made to the native genius.

Phuley as genuine *mahatma*: Gandhi perhaps was the first person in India to use religion to fight a political war. He used this weapon with dreadful effect. He permanently diverted the attention of the people from their pressing problems. What they wanted was a socio-economic liberation from the bondage of caste system- untouchability, male domination, feudal oppression and preistcraft. But Gandhi told them that the British was their real enemy, thereby hiding their immediate and more serious caste oppressors. India's urban-based Hindu big business and the rural-based upper caste feudal oppressors wanted exactly this. They saw in Gandhi their god. They wanted somebody to divert the wrath of the enraged masses away from them. So, these oppressors backed Gandhi to the hilt. They financed him and the media they owned built myths around him. They conferred the highest title - *mahatma* - on him, though much earlier people as a whole conferred the title of *mahatma* on Maharashtra's Jyotirao Phuley, a guru of Dr. Babasaheb Ambedkar. *Mahatma* Phuley was the India's genuine and the only *Mahatma* while Gandhi was a fake. The upper caste exploiters were the first to wear *khadi* (home-spun cloth) and praised him. Gandhi diverted the attention of the people to non-issues like non-drinking, non-killing of cows, vegetarianism, urine therapy and all sorts of nonsense. Religion in India has been always the tool of the oppressors. But nobody in India has used it so effectively as Gandhi.

If "Sacred Brahmins" like Tilak and Godse had their way they would have destroyed Hinduism by confronting the masses, by sharpening the caste contradicitons. But Gandhi cunningly thwarted such a confrontation and killed even minor contradictions. He instead mingled with them, said the *Harijans* were his chosen children, Muslims his darling and put on plastic smiles. He deceived everybody with sweet words.

When thinkers and scholars, writers and journalists in the West witnessed this "gandhian miracle"moving millions of slumbering, half-starved masses, they started reassessing Hinduism. They all attributed this to the "inherent strength of Hinduism."

Walking naked in London: It was only when a bare-bodied Gandhi came to London in his loin clothes that they got a real shock of their lives. Of late dress might have lost much of its importance. One can dress any way one likes - even on a formal occasion. But that was not the case when Gandhi went to London. Churchill, the then Prime Minister of UK, called him contemptuously a half-naked fakir. None had the courage to defy dress regulations in those days particularly in London. One has to be dressed in a particular way for a particular occasion. There used to be a dinner dress, office-dress, evening dress, dancing dress, funeral dress etc. And anybody who slightly deviated from these conservative rules in the convention-ridden England of those days used to be an object of ridicule. None had the courage to violate these social customs, Gandhi perhaps was the first person in the history of England (at that time London was the capital of the whole world) to violate this rule and shock the conservative English world.

He came in his loin-cloth facing a battery of cameramen. As Londoners gazed at him with dismay, he walked with full confidence, holding his head high. There was not even a twinkle of hesitation in his eyes. It was in the same London that he used to go about in his formal dress. The Western world was under the impression that he was a lunatic like many others in India. But when he came in bare body, loin-cloth, the West thought it was the "Hindu spirituality" that gave him that inner strength. It was this supreme confidence of Gandhi that gave the Western world an entirely new vision of Hinduism. Gandhi, whom they considered essentially a Hindu monk, was walking almost naked in London - that too in public, and that too when coming to meet the British Prime Minister. From where did he get this courage? They thought it was the religion that he professed that gave him that supreme confidence. Otherwise, how dare he go about half-naked in that dress? Gandhi caught the international attention and the Western world attributed his courage and confidence entirely to Hinduism, its "mysticism", its "inner spiritual strength".

Hinduism moves West: From then onwards they completely changed their opinion on Hinduism and India. They started thinking that Hinduism was a religion that gifted one with tremendous spiritual power. Gandhi would not have had the courage to defy the established Western customs and manners had he not been charged with that supreme spiritual power of Hinduism. Gandhi mesmerised the West for the first time. Therefore, the credit for bringing respectability to India and Hinduism goes to Gandhi. The Westerners started thinking that Hinduism indeed was a unique religion that could move masses. If Gandhi had roused the whole lot of hungry, illiterate masses of Indians against the British, it might be surely due to Hinduism. They started admiring Hinduism only because of Gandhi.

A fire-fighter: If Gandhi had not come on the scene, the "freedom struggle" against the British would have taken a socio-economic shape and this would have resulted in a major revolution - perhaps like the Russian or Chinese Revolution or even greater than that. But right at that time Gandhi came like a fire-fighter. Here and there India did catch fire. And Gandhi rushed wherever there was fire like a typical fire-fighter driving his firebrigade vehicle, and extinguished the fire. He used Hinduism very effectively to fight the fire of socio-economic struggles. When the peoples' wrath reached unmanageable proportions, he knew that they would take to violence leading to the destruction of the exploiters. To curb such a socio-economic struggle, he used his threat to fast-unto-death. So Gandhi was a typical fire-fighter. He never created fire. Rather, he extinguished the fire for which he was not responsible. A fire-fighter needs fire. Then only he comes on the scene and extinguishes the fire. A fire-fighter will be jobless if there is no fire.

What India needed then (and also now) was a leader who would create more fire that would burn the whole land - like Lenin in USSR and Mao in China. But Gandhi like a true counter-revolutionary came wherever there was fire and extinguished it and the water that he poured was Hinduism.

The entire country would have caught fire and in the fire not only the socio-economic liberation of the people would have taken place but in that fire the religion of Hinduism, which held us in bondage, would have been roasted alive. But Gandhi, the fire-fighter, saved Hinduism from sure death, killed the Indian revolution, and handed over the country to a Brahmin-Bania imperialism that proved worse than the British imperialism. That is why we find Gandhi's photo in every police-station, the symbol of tyranny.

X - WHY & HOW GANDHI WENT TO MASSES ?

Gandhi's two greatest opponents were Dr. Babasaheb Ambedkar and M.A. Jinnah. India's tallest Muslim leader, Jinnah, opposed Gandhi on every front, political, statesmanship and ideology and Babasaheb opposed him in statesmanship and ideology. Babasaheb could not politically oppose Gandhi because Gandhi held no political office. Gandhi had neither a cadre-based leadership nor organised followers just as Jinnah had. Dalits in those days could not be organised as a political force because of their total illiteracy, poverty, wide dispersal in villages scattered all over India and lack of ideology and therefore, Babasaheb had to remain content only with his legal and constitutional expertise in which he had no equals in the whole of India. That is how both Babasaheb and Jinnah never violated the law of the land but achieved their objectives solely through constitutional means. The only two occasions when both resorted to mass agitations were the Mahad agitation by Babasaheb and the "Direct Action Day" in Calcutta by Jinnah in August 1946.

Against Hindus not British: Both these agitations were directed against the Hindus and not against the British Government.Babasaheb had another handicap that there were not sufficient Dalit voters to back him as the voting rights were restricted in those days only to the educated, property-holders and tax-payers, unlike the adult franchise (under the present Constitution) which enables every citizen above 18 years of age to vote. Dalit consciousness was also too low when compared to what it is now when Dalit Dr. Ambedkar movement has turned out to be the country's single biggest movement.

Under this provision of restricted franchise, the 35% Muslim population had then 35% votes. There were many educated, property-holders and tax-payers among Muslims. In contrast, the Dalits were uneducated, almost 100% propertyless and hence non-tax payers. So, Dalits had virtually no voting strength. As against this, the 15%

Hindus (Brahmins as educated, Kshatriyas and Banias as tax-payers and property-holders) had the rest of the 60% voting power. Sikhs, Parsis, Anglo-Indians and Indian Christians though with lesser voting strength (altogether 5%) could get representation through reserved constituencies.

Separate electorate: Since Babasaheb was black-mailed by Gandhi to give up the demand for separate electorate for Dalits through his treacherous "Poona Pact", he even lost the whip with which he could threaten the Hindus. The only weapon he could use, therefore, was the weapon of his super-human intellectual power and his constitutional expertise.

Apart from this political setup, the system of Indian governance then was pure bureaucracy and everything was done as per the rule of law. The highest authority in India then was the Governor-General who used to be a top British bureaucrat. He used to be selected from among a few very well-trained experts on everything about India and Indians. They used to be perfect in their knowledge about India's history, geography, religions, national identities and aspirations of the various factions, culture, linguistic differences. They used to have offices at the district and taluk level who would know everything and about every activity, aspiration and programme of all people in their respective areas. A telephone call by the Governor-General's secretary any officer at any time would provide all the necessary information about everything from every area. They had ready references, which were like dictionaries, which would provide every information about every village in British India. Any discussion with the Governor-General on any matter could not be on assumption and imagination. There could be no vague assertions and suggestion. Everything had to be with mathematical accuracy.

Experts on India: Apart from this expertise of the Governor-General, the only authority to whom he was answerable was the Secretary of State for India, who used to be yet another bureaucrat sitting in London, along with other Secretaries of States for Burma, Ceylon, Australia, etc., which were the other parts of the British Empire. This "Secretary of State for India" was answerable to "Secretary of States", who was answerable to the Prime Minister of England. The Secretary of State for India sitting in London used to be a greater expert on India and Indians than the Governor-General of India. As bureaucrats, all these officers believed in the rule of law, and sternly followed the rule book. Any amount of urging, entreating, pleasing, threatening and coercion would not bend them. The only thing that could make them change their decision or take new decisions could be better information, solid facts and reasoning. Agitations and violation of the laws were matters of law and order which could be just routine matters.

Both Babasaheb and Jinnah being experts not only in law and constitution but were also experts in the knowledge that the Governor-General himself had on India and Indians and could defeat, astound and convince him about their version and repudiate the Governor-General's version. If the Governor-General did not yield, they had the capacity to convince his superior, the Secretary of State for India and his boss, the Secretary of States, upon which the Governor-General would get a bad remark in his service record. So from the Governor-General's level itself discussions used to be in the most academic manner, entirely on solid facts and figures. Both Jinnah and Babasaheb had the stature, commanding personality and expertise to discuss with any British bureaucratic authority any time and convince him of their viewpoints.

Seervai's verdict on partition: Minutes of their discussions used to be all recorded and the letters written by them are parts of the official files, which have been recently released from the India Office Library, London, which speak of their unmatchable knowledge.

Some such minutes, letters, telegrams, telephonic talks etc. relating to the partition of India have been dug out by H.M. Seervai, the eminent Parsi jurist, and included in his book, *Partition of India - Myth and Reality*, which are hundred percent true and fix the entire responsibility of partition on Gandhi, Nehru and Patel. (DV Editorial March 1, 1983: "*Gandhi vs. Dr. Ambedkar*").

Muslim League in Jinnah's pocket: So both Babasaheb and Jinnah having understood the monolithic, bureaucratic setup and its weaknesses spent most of their time in reading books in their study and fully equipped themselves to face and defeat the bureaucrats. They had the patience, the selflessness and the IQ to read, understand and digest information and suggest improvements and alternations, and commanded the highest respect with the authorities for their command over the subject and the representative character of their view. Jinnah used to say that the entire office of the Muslim League was in his brief case. He had the humility to avoid saying "in his head". Since he had a powerful, well organised political party, hc could say "in my brief case". Babasaheb could not say even that because he had no such organised political party but spent his every minute reading and writing for future generations and said, "while Jinnah and Gandhi could sleep peacefully at night, because their people were awake, I have to remain awake, read and write all the night, as my people are asleep". (DV July 16, 1988 p.8: "*Gandhi-Jinnah & Dr. Ambedkar : Their role in history*", Shankaranand Shastri, New Delhi). So, Jinnah could act both as a politician and statesman, bothering both about next general election as politician and about the next generation as statesman whereas Babasaheb had to remain content with his being a statesman worrying only about the next generation.

Proud Bhoodevatas: As against this, Gandhi was not a man of knowledge, not to speak of being an expert. Not only Gandhi, not a single follower of Gandhi had any expertise. The proud *Bhoodevatas*, the very embodiment of wisdom having been created from the head of Brahma, their Creator, could not produce a single expert and, therefore, handed over the responsibility to a third-grade creature, a Bania, born out of the *papa yoni*, and remained satisfied with becoming his followers, admirers, agents and propagandists, because they thought he was the greatest *Chanakya* of the time. This Gandhi, as the *Modern*

Chanakya, without any knowledge of modern arts and sciences, strictly followed the great *Chanakyan* tricks and went to the Hindu masses and roused them against the British government, got their own properties destroyed through boycott of British goods, set fire to government property, instigated them to discard their degrees, government jobs, give up studies, resort to killing of Muslims and Dalits, and all sorts of mass agitations, salt-satyagraha etc - all kinds of gimmicks - all kinds of violence in the name of non-violence.

King of Banias: The greatest asset of Gandhi was neither knowledge nor leadership but his Bania caste through which he established contacts with the financial empire of Banias and made G.D. Birla the king of Banias. He convinced his *jatwalas* that Banias would be the biggest beneficiaries if the British were to quit India. He assured them that after independence he would force a ban on foreign goods, and British firms would be compelled to sell 51% of their shares to Indians and these shares would be purchased by Banias through the loans advanced by Indian Banks, which would receive loans from the Reserve Bank and to provide money to the Reserve Bank, money would be borrowed by the Government of India from every country of the world. The Government of India would become the agent of the Banias if the future rulers of India are purchased right now by providing huge funds to the Congress Party through him. Such funds donated to the Congress through him would make the Congress Party entirely dependent upon him and he would become the country's dictator. This was the game plan of Gandhi.

The miserly Banias, groaning under the caste curse of *vaidiks*, quickly realised the benefits of this grand design of the *mahatma*, their *jati* leader, and started paying any amount of money that Gandhi would demand. Never before their *jati* had produced a leader who made even the *vaidiks* to dance to his tunes.

The Congress Party, which used to conduct its sessions in palatial mansions of retired bureaucrats, rich lawyers, loyal rajas, started grand sessions every year in open maidans for days together, in different cities of India, to which people would flock from every part of India in groups, the travelling and incidental expenses of the people being met by their local leaders, who in turn would receive money directly from the party funds or from the agents of Birlas.

All sorts of food, vegetarian and meat, were served to delegates and pretty women acted as hosts. After enjoying the fun for two-three days, the delegates used to return to their places and received honour from the Bania agents and projected as leaders. The delegates travelled in rail in third class, the local leaders in second class and the top leaders in first class. Even the incidental expenses were paid according to the class.

Publicity-seeking stunts: Besides, Gandhi had created a large number of publicity-seeking institutions, like Gandhi Ashram, Gandhi Seva Sangh, Harijan Seva Sangh, Hindi Prachar Sabha etc., and also appointed a large number of deputy gandhis and deputy *mahatmas* who were all confirmed cardinals of gandhism, believers in the gandhian principle and gandhian dictatorship, carriers of his message and executors of his orders. He also had regional gandhis like "Bengal Gandhi", "Maharashtra Gandhi", "Gujarat Gandhi" etc., and also a "Frontier Gandhi" (Khan Abdul Ghaffar Khan) whose duty it was to convert the martial Pathans to vegetarianism and non-violence.

All these deputy gandhis and gandhian institutions, were provided with ample funds by the Gujarat and Bombay Banias as they were sure to protect and promote the Bania economic interests in post-"independent" India.

These developments were being carefully observed by Babasaheb who feared that India's "independence" would only mean transfer of power from the British capitalist to the hands of more dangerous Indian capitalists and the Indian Bania would destroy India and Indians since as against the British capitalist who believed in the principle of manufacture and sale of the best possible goods at competitive rates, the Indian Bania believed not in manufacture, but in purchase and hoarding of goods, raising its prices and selling it in blackmarket. The Banias took every word and advice of Gandhi and pumped huge funds as any secure investment in the Congress Party was sure to fetch them huge dividends. The Bania were very suitably rewarded after "independence" and half of India's wealth has gone to the pocket of this half-a-per cent of Indian Bania population. Neither Jinnah nor Babasaheb could get such fund-providers as Gandhi could, nor could they give promises of reward in future. Their only asset was their scholarship and intellectual honesty, using which they could help as few people as they have helped. Gandhi did not have even that most elementary wisdom that lies and *chanakyan* tricks will not last as long as Truth and Honesty. That is why we see in India gandhism is rotting, and Ambedkerism is rising day by day.

XI - INDIAN HISTORY AS A CLASH BETWEEN GODSES & GANDHIS

This book should not be taken as a verdict on Godse or the Hindu nazi para-military force RSS but a pen-picture of the power of the Hindu revivalism which is taking new and newer shape. Even marxism of the Indian brand looks like an attempt at revivalism. It is this adaptability, its terrible resilience that has made Hinduism survive every earthquake.

It is only the Gandhis ("Socialist Brahmins") who give Hinduism a new lease of life - not the Godses ("Sacred Brahmins"). Everytime Hinduism is threatened, it automatically throws up a Gandhi. Hence this book is not a verdict on those two remarkable individuals but two principal trends in Hindu history - two forces, pulls and pressures- that have always existed and will continue to exist as long as "Hinduism" lasts.

Godse represents those conservative, revivalist, "sacred", orthodox, backward-looking but honest Brahmins. And Gandhi (he was not a Brahmin but a Vaisya, belonging to the trading caste that is ranked third among the three twice-born *dwijas*) represents the dishonest, but called "progressive-socialist", sections. Both Godse and Gandhi belonged to the highest Hindu caste groups and represented less than 15% of the Hindu society. The entire history of Hinduism has been a perpetual war between these two forces. This "war" between these two forces is made to appear as an "ideological battle" between "progressive" and "conservative" forces.

Marxist-RSS fight: The beauty is that both the "rival" groups are led only by the Brahmins and which ever group gets defeated, it is only the Brahmins who will continue to rule India. The "war" between the two is made to appear so serious that those reading the Indian press, also owned and manned by the same ruling class, will get an impression that it is indeed a very genuine ideological difference that is making the "marxists" fight the RSS. But both of them are united in one thing - that is to keep the leadership of

India only in the hands of the Brahmins. But the vast masses of India comprising the Dalits, Backward Castes and even the persecuted minorities like the Muslims, Christians, Sikhs and Budhists are deceived and made to believe that this "clash" between the Godse and the Gandhi groups is nothing but a genuine, healthy, "ideological battle" raging in India. Having made them to come to this conclusion, the Dalits and other persecuted nationalities are then made to take sides and line up behind these two groups and then fight the battle on behalf of these two groups. While the masses fight and die, the ruling class remains united while putting on a false face of ideological difference. This is how the Dalits and the other persecuted nationalities are being fooled from centuries. There is no ideology in India. The only ruling ideology of India is "caste ideology". Even the "marxists" subscribe to it. They are Brahmins first, Brahmins second and Brahmins last.

Both Gandhi and Godse may be dead but the forces representing the two have been always there from the beginning of Hinduism and will continue to be there as long as Hinduism is there. Hence this book is more in the nature of an analysis of the complicated social forces in the bewildering maze that is India and not any commentary on these two individuals or any other individual. We have respect for both Godse and Gandhi as they did play a very important role in keeping the masses enthralled, making the slaves enjoy their slavery.

Jewish origin of Chitpavans: RSS is a thought with the facade of an organisation. It represents the Hindu nazi thought. This thought existed even before the RSS was born (1925). This thought will continue to exist even after the RSS is dead. So Godse, a Chitpavan, a tiny Brahmin caste group claiming Jewish origin [K.K. Gangadharan in the *Sociology of Revivalism*, Kalamkar Prakashan, New Delhi - 1970, quotes Linda Cox article in the *Illustrated Weekly*, 15.5.1970, p.6 to prove that the Chitpavan Brahmins were originally Jews, and adds that "historians and anthropologists also confirm their foreign origin", p.59. He adds that "Maureen Patterson who studied Chitpavan

Brahmin family histories has come to some tentative conclusions", p.107], came as representative of the Hindu nazis fully in keeping with the great traditions set by the Adi Shankara, a Namboodiri Brahmin of Kerala (Namboodiris came into Kerala around 700 AD). Therefore, Godse is not the end. Indira Gandhi outdid the RSS in Hindu revivalism as proved in the Jammu and Kashmir election (1983) and the earlier elections in Delhi. In the 1984 anti-Sikh riots of Delhi, it is the Congress leaders who led the attack on Sikhs killing thousands of Sikhs. P.V. Narasimha Rao, the living *Chanakya* and a Neogi Brahmin from Andhra Pradesh, demolished the Babri Masjid and pleased the entire upper caste world by goading them to loot and rob and himself becoming India's most corrupt Prime Minister. All these Hindu nazis parading as "Socialist Brahmins" are guided by the sole objective of keeping the Brahmins as India's ruling class. Brahminism thrives only on revivalism, falsification of history through the glorification of the past and finding scapegoats to divert the attention of Dalits, other "low caste" Hindus by telling them that their real enemies are Muslims, Christians, Sikhs.

Greatness of Ravana: Golwalkar had included the Dalits (Untouchables and Tribals) also in the list of his enemies. The Aryan fight against the *Rakshasas, Asuras, Daityas,Danavas, Pisachis* (demons) was nothing but a fight against the Dalits. Ravana was a Dalit leader of great virtue. Golwalkar in his book, *Bunch of Thoughts*, now and then refers to the *Rakshasas* and stresses the Hindu need to fight and destroy the *Rakshasas*. The three most famous Hindus festivals - Diwali, Holy, Dasara - are nothing but celebrations of destruction through burning of our great Ausara ancestors. Even to this day, the daily fighting that is going on in the country-side is nothing but an extension of this war between the Hindus and our people, *Rakshasas*. Let us be proud of the fact that we are *Rakshasas*. In the Vedas, the Brahmins described the indigenous peoples as *Rakshasas*.

Therefore, this book is a humble effort at warning our Dalit and other persecuted nationalities that as the Hindu India goes from one crisis to another, if not greater crisis, this Hindu nazi revivalism will take a more militant shape. We can be rest assured that Hindu India is in for a serious revivalist upsurge and in this fight of our people (Bahujan Samaj of the 85%), the "marxists", "ecologist" and "Socialist Brhamins" will side with the "Sacred Brahmins" by their silence and neutrality. India is heading for a caste and communal blood-bath and the ruling class is thirsting for our blood. The English-educated Hindu has become so intolerant, so bigoted, so hate-filled that he is forcing the Hindu government to wage a war against the Bahujans.

White Western racists join Hindu nazis: The beauty is that in this war between the two, the Hindu nazis have received support from the White Western racists who in their imaginary fear of the "Islamic fundamentalism" have stumbled upon the brahminical nazi philosophy as a panacea for their ills. The White Western racists are predicting a clash between the Cross (Christianity) and the Crescent (Islam) and taking advantage of this Western fear, India's Brahmins have assured the support of their swastika, *vedic* symbol. This is an entirely new and interesting development which neither Godse nor Gandhi ever dreamt of. Since Dalits and other persecuted nationalities are not in a position to stop this historic development, this surge, we can only take precautions to save ourselves from this ruling class violence. As the original inhabitants of India, we have a great responsibility to liberate India from these foreign exploiters and establish social justice.

Red carpet welcome to Hitler: So, a deep study of the principal Enemy is a must because we must remember that the Enemy that we are fighting is no ordinary Enemy. A set of people who fooled even the Germans, recognised as the most brilliant in the world, and even convinced them that Aryans were the ancestors of Germans, must be something extraordinary.(DV Dec. 16, 1996 p.9: "*Brahmin as a sociological wonder*"). The famous German indologist, Max Muller, called India a nation of philosophers. The world famous German philosopher, Schopenhauer, said that the "Vedas were the fruit of highest human knowledge and wisdom" (K.K. Gangadharan: *Sociology of Revivalism* - p. 35). That is how the Brahmins became the greatest admirers of Hitler and even sent him congratulatory telegrams expecting him to win the Second World War. In Calcutta, Madras, Poona and many other parts of India, they had planned a red-carpet welcome to Hitler on his victory. Brahmins claimed that the "Germans built their tremendous weapons from the recipes provided by those texts" (Hindu sacred scriptures like the Vedas).

Swastika gifted to nazis: Dr. Agehananda Bharati, in his article, "Hindu Scholars, Germany and Third Reich" (*Update*, Vol. 6 No.3, Sept. 1982 - Arhus, Denmark), says the Hindus considered Hitler as a *mahatma*. They were very proud that Hitler borrowed their symbol of swastika and made it the national flag of Germany. They were also happy that Sanskrit was made a compulsory subject in German schools, and Hitler, the *avatar*, was born to punish the British who brought sufferings to the Brhamins. (DV Oct. 1, 1996 p.10: "*Nazi philospher Nietzsche borrowed it from brahminism*" & DV April 16, 1997 p.20: "*Why Nietzsche rejected Christianity & followed brahminism*", Raju Thomas).

M.V. Kamath, a noted Brhamin journalist who served the *Times of India* as its Washington correspondent and later as editor of the *Illustrated Weekly*, is all praise for Germans while reviewing the book, *India's Road to Nationhood*, by Wilhem von Pochhamer, (Allied Publishers, Bombay) in the *Indian Express* (March 7, 1982). Kamath, who has been a regular columnist for Hindu nazi journals, cites the German author's praise for Brahmin "revolutionaries" like Tilak etc. For further references please read *The Aryan Myth* by Leon Paliakov, who shows how the Brahmins of India have fooled even the Germans and thus became the fathers of fascism (New American Library, 1974).

Father of fascism: When such is the ingenuity of the Enemy, it is our duty as the original inhabitants of this land and interested in the country's unity, integrity and prosperity to make a thorough study of the Enemy. If the world has produced a Hitler and a Mussolini, who together caused the Second World War, the origin and development of these two greatest fascist cult leaders of the world has to be traced to brahminism. Gangadharan in the *Sociology of Revivalism* (page 100 to 102) brings out the tremendous similarity between Hitlerism and the RSS. Therefore, the Fathers of Fascism are not the German philosophers but the Aryan invaders who imposed on us brahminism. (*Brahminism - Father of Fascism, Nazism, Racism* DSA, 1994). The Aryans thus naturally become the world enemies and tackling them becomes not only our concern but an international responsibility. To defend ourselves against such a formidable world Enemy, we have to fully equip ourselves, make a deep study of their fascist philosophy and both its Godses and Gandhis, who are two sides of the same coin. A humble effort is made in this work. To unravel its secrets and plan out an appropriate strategy, a deeper study of the Enemy and its philosophy is a must. Then only we can launch our liberation struggle.

Godse helped revolution: Every social movement, whether godseism (of the "Sacred Brahmins"), or gandhism (of the "Socialist Brhamins") is like a pendulum. When it swings to one extreme, it has to swing back to the other extreme. The social revolution launched by Jainism and Budhism produced a Godse in Adi Shankara. Reckless burning of widows as prescribed by Hinduism produced a Gandhi in Vivekananda and Raj Rammohan Roy. Long before the RSS was born, we had its forefathers in Tilak, Savarkar, Lala Lajpat Rai, Dayananda Saraswati etc. All of them were opposed to social justice and defended the caste system. They were honest enough to denounce secularism and democracy which are an anathema to Hinduism. When the pendulum swung to the other extreme, it produced a reaction and when the society was about to disintegrate at the time of the "freedom struggle" (which was nothing but a Brahmin-inspired struggle to drive out the British and replace it with the Brahmin-Bania rule) and a revolution was brewing, Gandhi came on the scene to give a new life to Hinduism by crushing the revolution. The Godse cult would have accelerated the revolution and India too would have had a Revolution like the one witnessed in China. But Gandhi frustrated the whole thing through his counter-revolutionary tactics. He poured cold water on the burning fire. Hence, from the point of view of sharpening of caste contradictions and the churning of the stinking, stagnant Hindu social cesspool, we must welcome the Godses and not the Gandhis. The Godses are our honest friends., We like the Godses.

Father of Hindu Nation: The Brahmins, Kshatriyas, Vaishyas and other top landed *shudra* castes, comprising the ruling class of Hindus, therefore,have to be ever grateful to Gandhi for checkmating this revolution. That is why Gandhi is called the "Father of the Nation". Father of which nation? Not ours. He is the father of their nation and not our nation. We have nothing against Gandhi. In fact, Gandhi's life was saved by our man - a Dalit. But for Babasaheb Ambedkar agreeing to sign the "Poona Pact", the *mahatma* would have died if he was honest in continuing his "Epic Fast". Kasturba, Gandhi's wife, came to Babasaheb and begged him to save her *mangala sutra* and Dr. Ambedkar reluctantly agreed. So, it was a Dalit who saved Gandhi but it was a Brahmin who killed Gandhi. In other words, Gandhi, the "Father of the Hindu nation", was killed by a Hindu only. Non-Hindus suffered under this father, who made them slaves and yet they did not retaliate. It is his own nation, his ungrateful nation, that bumped him off.

Gandhi was killed by a Hindu nazi party, RSS. This party might have succeeded in proving in the court that Godse was not in the RSS "at the time of killing Gandhi". We know how the courts, headed mostly by upper castes judges, function in Hindu India. These are the very judges who used the Supreme Court to promote Hinduism, denying reservations to Dalit converts to Christianity. These are the very judges who sought to destroy the Muslim identity through the Shah Banu case. These are the very judges who declared a centuries-old mosque at Faizabad (UP) as the Hindu god, Rama's birth place and said it is Hindu temple to be thrown open to worship disregarding Muslim sentiment and historical facts. These are the very judges who did everything to destroy the Mandal Commission recommendations to bring social justice to Backward Castes comprising 35% of our population. The courts in India with the exception of few judges are by and large anti-people and this is because they are not elected people. The Hindu nazis are using these very courts to break the Constitution that assures security to religious minorities. It is such a court that favoured the RSS.

Whenever any RSS man gets caught in a crime, it is a rule with the RSS to disown such a person. The judges, police, media, courts in this country being controlled by the upper caste Hindus, it is but natural that they were too willing to absolve Godse. But even a child tells in India that Gandhi was killed by the RSS (for more details read American CIA agent Curran's book on RSS, *Militant Hinduism in Indian Politics*, All-India Quami Ekta Sammelan; Delhi, 1970).

K.K. Gangadharan quotes Gopal Godse's articles in the Marathi weekly, *Sobat*, and S.S. Kanolkar's article in the *Mainstream* (July, 1970) to prove Nathuram Godse's RSS connections:

> Gopal Godse who has been released after completing his sentence in the Gandhi Murder Case, declares that both he and Nathuram belonged to the RSS. He is proud of the fact. He condemns the attitude of escapism adopted by the Jan Sangh in this respect. Godse boldly justifies both the facts that he and Nathuram belong to the RSS and it is they who were responsible for the Gandhi murder".

RSS should not turn dishonest: We don't know why the RSS is shy of admitting this fact. Such a historical blunder the RSS has committed will have to be regretted as the fast-changing waves of Indian history will one day force it to do so. RSS has a place in India as it represents a particular thought-the thought of the honest "Sacred Brahmins". If this is so, why should it be accused of dishonesty? Already the RSS is being accused of diluting its Hindu nazi philosophy, compromising on its fundamental principles in its race to win peoples' votes. The RSS, after having killed Gandhi, for sometime tried to flirt with its very enemy No. 1 - gandhism. RSS adopted the fake "gandhian socialism" as its philosophy with disastrous results, then it committed the most unpardonable blunder of amending its nazi philosophical book, *Bunch of Thoughts*. RSS sources tell us that lately its very sales have been stopped and attempts are being made to disown the book itself just as they disowned Godse who accomplished a historical task (V.T. Rajshekar: *Hinduism, Fascism and Gandhism - A Guide to every Intelligent Indian*, Dalit Sahitya Akademy, 1985).

Gandhi became a "martyr" by his assassination. RSS has thus helped Gandhi to shine by contrast. Whenever Hinduism is threatened, it automatically throws up a Godse and a Gandhi - each is complementary to the other. Godse helped Gandhi to become a martyr and Gandhi wanted Godse to deceive the starving millions of India. One cannot live without the other. If Godse is dangerous, Gandhi is more dangerous. Because Gandhi consolidated Hinduism. However, the Godses are our honest, open enemies but the Gandhis are our dishonest foes. With the Godses around, we can clearly see the Enemy. It is standing right before us, menacing. But the Gandhis are more dangerous because they come to us as our friends like a charming, smiling pretty girl and kill us with poison mixed in honey. An open enemy is any day better than a disguised enemy. Killing with a sweet smile is more dangerous, treacherous than torturing us by throwing us into a burning fire. Therefore, from the Dalit and persecuted nationalities' interest we welcome the Godses. The Godses rouse us to anger but the Gandhis kill our rage and make the slaves enjoy their slavery.

Puri temple entry: The Shankarachari of Puri is the best example of a "Sacred Brahmin". He told Indira Gandhi point blank that she could not be allowed inside the Puri Jagannath Temple as she was not a Hindu. The Prime

Minister tried several times and finally she died - her wish remaining unfulfilled. He never relented just because she was the Prime Minister of the country. "Sacred Brahmins" never hide their hatred against Dalits. They are uncompromising. They say the Untouchables have no brains, and therefore, they are fit to be slaves. "Socialist Brahmins" say "reservations" must be given to Dalits because of centuries of deprivation. When the "Socialist Brahmins" say this, Dalits vote wholesale to such "Socialist Brahmins" and that makes the upper castes to come to power. So, it is the "Sacred Brahmins" who help "Socialist Brhamins" to rule us. They have a secret understanding between themselves. The Godses administer morphine only to a single individual patient who cannot bear the pain but the Gandhis put an entire population to mass hypnotism. Both quarrel in public but share the spoils in secret. They fight during the day but dine and sleep in the same bed when night falls. All over India, the Dalits, Tribals, BCs, Muslims, Christians and Sikhs are under the leadership of the "Socialist Brhamins" having been deceived by their sweet-sounding slogan. Beware of the "Socialist Brahmins."

Schizophrenic people? Be that as it may, we have to scientifically plan out our strategy. If India has to be liberated, both the Godses and Gandhis have to be eliminated. This can be done only by using the Godses against the Gandhis and allowing the Godses to remain in India - but fully reined in and yet their human rights fully protected with reservations assured in proportion to their population. We fully realise the seige mentality threatening them. The *vaidik* vampire has become extremely suspecious. It feels threatened. This is the one and the only case in the world where the unquestioned monarch of a country is feeling insecure. Thinking sections among *vaidiks* are not getting sound sleep in the night. Quite a number of our professional colleagues have confessed this. Theirs is the only one case of its kind in the world. *Vaidiks* are the rulers of India and owners of its property, enjoying all the pleasure, posts and perks. Yet they are uneasy, insecure and deeply worried. They are afraid of whom? We are the slaves, paupers, penniless. That means they are guilty of something. Quite a number of *vaidiks* continue to be "poor" and "unemployed". Their own "sacred scriptures" have not solved their problems. There is something basically wrong with these people. Is it schizophrenic? We don't know what it is. It needs a deep research by a foreign psychiatrist. But can the country afford to suffer just because a very small section of negligible size has turned suicide-prone? Is it not our duty, as owners of this land, to save India and the suicide-prone?

This task of saving India needs tremendous knowledge, wisdom, skill, strategy and planning. It has to be accomplished before the "Gandhian Era" ends with the end of the 20th century - only two years away. The 21st century shall be the "Dr. Ambedkar Era". We have been repeatedly telling this. At the beginning of the 21st century, Dalits will have to take over the leadership of the Indian Revolution. Time is running out. Therefore, we call upon the Dalits to hurry up. Dalit intellectuals have a big role. It is they who have to lead. And before launching the war, it is they who have to study the Godses and Gandhis. Hence this book, *Why Godse Killed Gandhi?*

❁ ❁ ❁ ❁

ANNEXURE

WHY THOSE WHO KILLED GANDHI BARK AT THOSE WHO CRITICISE GANDHI? A BRAHMINICAL PUZZLE

In the last week of December 1996, our "national" toilet papers owned and run by the ruling brahminical forces tried to make a big "controversy" out of a statement of fact made by Hindu Nazi Shiv Sena chief Bal Thackeray on M.K. Gandhi, the "Father of the Hindu nation". This is what he said:

> "Gandhiji was always accompanied by two girls. Yet that was OK with everyone. If we do something we are criticised. Gandhiji's *brahmacharya* (celibacy) was a fraud, he said this addressing a meeting near Aurangabad. Thackeray then sniggered: "Nowadays nobody even remembers Gandhi". (*Hindustan Times* Dec. 28, '96).

Another Hindu nazi leader Pramod Mahajan of the *Brahman Jati Party* supported Thackeray and said:

> **Mumbai:** "I do not feel that Gandhiji was the father of the nation. Gandhi is a great son of the nation. But to call him father of the nation is not valid as India was not born in 1947 but has a history of 5000 years", said BJP general secretary Pramod Mahajan. He made this statement at a joint press conference with Sena supremo Bal Thackeray on Friday. BJP does not consider Gandhi as the father of the nation. (*Hindustan Times* Jan.4, '97).

Now, the point to be noted is that these "derogatory" statements on Gandhi are not made by any Dalit leader or *Dalit Voice*. Our people have every reason to be angry with Gandhi because it was he who came in the way of Babasaheb's efforts to give separate electorate to Dalits with his infamouse fast that ended with the notorious "Poona Pact" (1932) that sealed the fate of Dalits.

Sleeping with girls: The "derogatory" statements were made by two top Hindu leaders - one a Kayasth (Thackeray) and another a Brahmin. And yet the brahminical press directed its venomous attacks only at Thackeray but not

Mahajan. The reason is obvious. In DV itself we had long back published a noted authority's article on Gandhi sleeping naked with young girls. The article had then come as a shock to our readers. (DV Aug. 1, 1991 p.17, Bhikku Parekh: "*Gandhi, a sex maniac?*"). But these are historical facts. The *Telegraph* (Jan.18, '97) published an article by Arvind Kala detailing Gandhi's "sex experiments" with young girls. He lists the writings of Nirmal Kumar Bose (*My Days With Gandhi*) who worked with Gandhi during 1946-47. Kala says Lary Collins and Dominique Lapierre also recorded in the *Freedom at Midnight* that many leaders had warned Gandhi against sleeping naked with Manu, his own 19-year-old grandniece and constant companion.

Arvind Kala then adds:

> "Thackeray has done great service to India by reopening a part of Gandhi's life that Indians never discuss out of misplaced loyalty to Gandhi."

Gandhi's association with young women in his last years has been documented by several writers. Margaret Bourke-White, a photographer of the *Life* magazine in her book, *Half Way to Freedom*, says "In 1946, Gandhi used to receive a daily two-hour massage from Dr. Sushila Nayar or one of the other women in his ashram.

Amrit Kaur goes mad: Ronald Segal in his book, *Crisis in India*, says "Gandhi's close connection with women was frequently harmful to them. Many became neurotic. One was Raj Kumari Amrit Kaur, India's first Health Minister. Gandhi took his bath naked in full view of women. He had his daily massage virtually naked with young girls." Both Nehru and Sardr Patel were furious with Gandhi and had lodged strong complaints but Gandhi never bothered. All these are facts of history.

If so, why the brahminical forces are so furious when these facts are disclosed? This is a very important point that again pinpoints how these *vaidik* brahminical forces take advantage of the law of contradictions to confuse and befool the people of India.

Gandhi's murder: If the brahminical forces of India

have such blind admiration for Gandhi and hailed him as a *mahatma* and "Father of the Nation", why a respected Pune *vaidik* of the Hindu nazi organisation, RSS, killed him and the Hindu nazis distributed sweets on the day Gandhi was killed?

How can the Hindu nazi forces kill the very person they worship? How and why they resort to both mutually contradictory actions? This important point is discussed in this leader.

Gopal Godse book: Gandhi was not killed by a Muslim, Dalit or even a Backward Caste. Not even by an upper caste Hindu. He was killed by a Pune Chitpavan Brahmin. If a Muslim or a Dalit had killed Gandhi,as they had a real goruse against him and as he had ruined their lives, we could well understand it.

Victims of Gandhi and gandhism did not kill him. He was killed by a person whose *vaidik* vampire was benefitted to the maximum by him. This is the puzzle of the law of contradictions.

Gopal Godse, younger brother of Nathuram Godse who killed Gandhi on Jan.30, 1948 in Delhi, recently released a book, *Why I Assassinated Mahatma Gandhi?* The brahminical "national" toilet papers gave Gopal Godse and his press conference wide coverage with his picture and also that of the book. Many dailies and journals interviewed Gopal Godse and showered praises for his "dedication". *Vaidik* leaders in India had not called for a ban on that book. Rather, the book was a bestseller and received good reviews. If the brahminical rulers are great gandhians and frown at any attack on Gandhi, why Godse and his book are extolled? This is the million dollar puzzle. Even now, on every Jan.30, the Hindu nazi *chaddi* party celebrates the day and extolls the Gandhi-killer Godse. Is this not strange?

Killing & then praising: Here lies the greatness in the *vaidik* behaviour. They only kill Gandhi and after killing him, they only praise him and persecute those who criticise him. Thackeray became one such victim of *vaidik* wrath for having stated the facts about Gandhi's sex life. Why do the *vaidiks* behave in this strange, unexplainable way? Why this self-contradictory behaviour? This is where the law of contradictions come to our rescue. The *vaidik* forces being experts on the law of contradictions and in managing the contradicitons, they know how to make the best use of the contradictions.

Founder of Hindu Rashtra: The *vaidiks* carried Gandhi on their heads, paraded him and conferred upon him the highest title because nobody in India has done so much to promote the *vaidik* interests, including installing a *vaidik* as India's first Prime Minister. If India has already become a *Hindu Rashtra*, it was Gandhi who did everything to promote it. So, they have to be ever grateful to Gandhi for protecting and promoting brahminical interests.

They don't like anybody disturbing these values - the foundation on which their *sanatana* system stands. That is why when non-Brahmins like Thackeray criticise Gandhi and gandhism *vaidik* forces howl at these people and pounce upon them even if facts are spoken.

Riddle of Rama and Krishna: The published facts about Gandhi also have the full sanction of the *sanatana* system. Almost all Hindu gods displayed the same character (Dr. B.R. Ambedkar - *Riddles of Rama and Krishna*, DSA, 1995). So, when non-*vaidiks* criticise Gandhi and gandhism it naturally hurts the Hindu feelings and sentiments because gandhim is nothing but sugar-coated Hinduism. The credit for promoting, perfecting and establishing the *Hindu Rashtra* goes to Gandhi rather than the RSS-BJP.

That is why whenever a non-*vaidik* criticises Gandhi and gandhism *vaidiks* pounce upon them like mad dogs.

M.K. Gandhi today is forgotten and crying from the dustbin of history for attention. Gandhian literature has no buyers. The Gandhi Samadhi in Delhi is visited only by visiting VIPs for purposes of photogrpah. The mass of people never enter this place. Even on Gandhi's birth anniversary, which is a public holiday, the people as such do not evince any interest. But the *vaidik* ruling class makes it a big event by giving a big media buildup to frighten the public. Within 50 years of "independence", people of India have discarded Gandhi. The rising star is Dr. Babasaheb Ambedkar who is most hated by the brahminical forces. This is also a fact of history. But India's monopoly media in the hands of these very same brahminical forces will never, ever allow the truth to see the light of the day. Such suppression of facts too has the full sanction of the *sanatana* system.

Be that as it may, the *vaidik* Hindu nazi forces are trying to rule India by using the law of contradictions to their advantage. But how long? History alone has the answer.

*(**Dalit Voice** Editorial Feb. 16-28, 1997)*